譯自中國文

TRANSLATIONS FROM THE CHINESE

by Arthur Waley

ILLUSTRATED BY
CYRUS LE ROY BALDRIDGE

New York: Alfred A. Knopf: Mcmxli

Preface by Arthur Waley

THERE ARE one or two questions which readers of ancient Chinese poetry, translated into another language, are bound to ask. Is it really at all like our poetry? Does it scan, does it rhyme? The answer to these questions is that (compared, for example, with Japanese poetry) Chinese traditional poetry is very similar to ours. Its lines have a fixed number of syllables and rhyme is obligatory; so that old Chinese poetry strongly resembles traditional English verse, and is not at all like the free verse of Europe and America today.

Modern Chinese poets have of course experimented in free verse; but the tendency is always to come back to rhyme and strict form. Most of the poems in this book are either in lines of five syllables or in lines of seven syllables all the way through. In the English, so far as possible, a stress represents each syllable; so that a Chinese reader will easily recognize the metre of the original. I have not used rhyme, because what is really, in the long run, of most interest to American readers is what the poems say; and if one uses rhyme, it is impossible not to sacrifice sense to sound. For the same reason, I have chosen poems which say something interesting. Those are the ones that translate best. It does not at all follow that they rank highest as poetry in the original; but with very few exceptions the poems in this book are by poets whom the Chinese themselves have always greatly admired. I have not attempted to set up any new gods.

And now a word about the subjects with which the poems deal. The most conspicuous feature of European poetry is its pre-occupation with love. This is apparent not only in actual "love-poems," but in all poetry where the personality of the writer is in any way obtruded. The poet tends to exhibit himself in a romantic light; in fact, to recommend himself as a lover.

The Chinese poet has a tendency different but analogous. He recommends himself not as a lover, but as a friend. He poses as a person of infinite leisure (which we should most like our friends to possess) and free from worldly ambitions (which constitute the greatest bars to friendship). He would have us think of him as a boon companion, a great drinker of wine, who will not disgrace a social gathering by quitting it sober.

To the European poet the relation between man and woman is a thing of supreme importance and mystery. To the average Chinese poet it is something commonplace, obvious—a need of the body, not a satisfaction of the *emotions*. These he reserves entirely for friendship. I have been criticized for saying something like this; but the vast mass of classical Chinese poetry amply confirms my view. Accordingly we find that while our poets tend to lay stress on physical courage and other qualities normally admired by women, Po Chü-i is not ashamed to write such a poem as "Alarm at entering the Gorges." Our classical poets imagine themselves very much as Art has portrayed them—bareheaded and wild-eyed, with shirts unbuttoned at the neck as though they feared that a seizure of emotion might at any minute suffocate them. The Chinese poet tends to introduce himself as a timid recluse, "Reading the Book of Changes at the Northern Window," playing chess with a Taoist priest, or practising calligraphy with an occasional visitor.

I do not mean to say that the gentle and reflective attitude traditional in Chinese poetry in any way gives us a key to the whole of Chinese life. Martial vigour, administrative ability, romantic love, all played their part; but in the whole bulk of classical poetry, say from the seventh to the fourteenth century, how minute a proportion for a moment touches any of these themes!

And now the translater must add a line or two of self-defence. The translations here printed were made over twenty years ago. Since then my own knowledge of Chinese and the general study of it in America and Europe have made enormous progress. In arranging the poems for this illustrated edition I have corrected a certain number of mistakes. But on the whole I have reprinted the poems as they stood in 1918 and 1919. There is a great deal that specialists might quarrel with; but not much, I hope, that will be definitely misleading to the general public. To understand unfailingly anything written a thousand years and more ago is not easy; but my Chinese friends have generally assured me that these translations come pretty close to the original; closer, they have sometimes been kind enough to say, than those of any other translater.

Contents

POEMS BY PO CHÜ-I

Translations from the Chinese

Battle

By Ch'ü Yüan (332–295 B.C.?)

Author of the famous poem "Li Sao"
or "Falling into Trouble"

Finding that he could not influence the conduct of his prince, he drowned himself in the river Mi-lo. The modern Dragon Boat Festival is supposed to be in his honour.

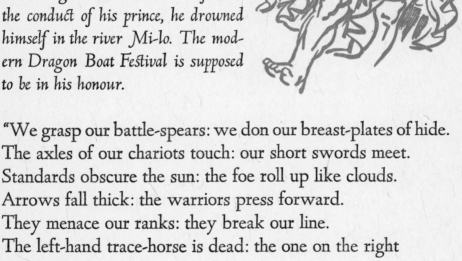

"We grasp our battle-spears: we don our breast-plates of hide.
The axles of our chariots touch: our short swords meet.
Standards obscure the sun: the foe roll up like clouds.
Arrows fall thick: the warriors press forward.
They menace our ranks: they break our line.
The left-hand trace-horse is dead: the one on the right
  is smitten.
The fallen horses block our wheels: they impede the
  yoke-horses!"

3

They grasp their jade drum-sticks: they beat the
    sounding drums.
Heaven decrees their fall: the dread Powers are angry.

The warriors are all dead: they lie on the moor-field.
They issued but shall not enter: they went but shall
    not return.
The plains are flat and wide; the way home is long.
Their swords lie beside them: their black bows, in their hand.

Though their limbs were torn, their hearts could not
    be repressed.
They were more than brave: they were inspired with the
    spirit of "Wu".[1]
Steadfast to the end, they could not be daunted.
Their bodies were stricken, but their souls have taken
    Immortality—
Captains among the ghosts, heroes among the dead.

[1] I.e., military genius.

4

The Man-Wind
and the Woman-Wind

*A "fu", or prose-poem, by Sung Yü (fourth century B. C.)
nephew of Ch'ü Yüan.*

HSIANG, king of Ch'u, was feasting in the Orchid-tower Palace, with Sung Yü and Ching Ch'ai to wait upon him. A gust of wind blew in and the king bared his breast to meet it, saying: "How pleasant a thing is this wind which I share with the common people." Sung Yü answered: "This is the Great King's wind. The common people cannot share it." The king said: "Wind is a spirit of Heaven and Earth. It comes wide spread and does not choose between noble and base or between high and low. How can you say 'This is the king's wind'?" Sung answered: "I have heard it taught that in the crooked lemon-tree birds make their nests and to empty spaces winds fly. But the wind-spirit that comes to different things is not the same." The king said: "Where is the wind born?" and Sung answered: "The wind is born in the ground. It rises in the extremities of the green p'ing-flower. It pours into the river-valleys and rages at the mouth of the pass. It follows the rolling flanks of Mount T'ai and dances beneath the pine-trees and cypresses. In gusty bouts it whirls. It rushes in fiery anger. It rumbles low with a noise like thunder, tearing down rocks and trees, smiting forests and grasses.

5

"But at last abating, it spreads abroad, seeks empty places and crosses the threshold of rooms. And so growing gentler and clearer, it changes and is dispersed and dies.

"It is this cool clear Man-Wind that, freeing itself, falls and rises till it climbs the high walls of the Castle and enters the gardens of the Inner Palace. It bends the flowers and leaves with its breath. It wanders among the osmanthus and pepper-trees. It lingers over the fretted face of the pond, to steal the soul of the hibiscus. It touches the willow leaves and scatters the fragrant herbs. Then it pauses in the courtyard and turning to the North goes up to the Jade Hall, shakes the hanging curtains and lightly passes into the inner room.

"And so it becomes the Great King's wind.

"Now such a wind is fresh and sweet to breathe and its gentle murmuring cures the diseases of men, blows away the stupor of wine, sharpens sight and hearing and refreshes the body. This is what is called the Great King's wind."

The king said: "You have well described it. Now tell me of the common people's wind." Sung said: "The common people's wind rises from narrow lanes and streets, carrying clouds of dust. Rushing to empty spaces it attacks the gateway, scatters the dust-heap, sends the cinders flying, pokes among foul and rotting things, till at last it enters the tiled windows and reaches the rooms of the cottage. Now this wind is heavy and turgid, oppressing man's heart. It brings fever to his body, ulcers to his lips and dimness to his eyes. It shakes him with coughing; it kills him before his time.

"Such is the Woman-Wind of the common people."

6

The following is a sample of Sung Yü's prose:

Master Tēng-t'u

By Sung Yü (third century B. C.)

ONE DAY when the Chamberlain, master Tēng-t'u, was in attendance at the Palace he warned the King against Sung Yü, saying: "Yü is a man of handsome features and calm bearing and his tongue is prompt with subtle sentences. Moreover, his character is licentious. I would submit that your Majesty is ill-advised in allowing him to follow you into the Queen's apartments." The King repeated Tēng-t'u's words to Sung Yü. Yü replied: "My beauty of face and calmness of bearing were given me by Heaven. Subtlety of speech I learnt from my teachers. As for my character, I deny that it is licentious." The King said: "Can you substantiate your statement that you are not licentious? If you cannot, you must leave the Court." Sung Yü said: "Of all the women in the world, the most beautiful are the women of the land of Ch'u. And in all the land of Ch'u there are none like the women of my own village. And in my village there are none that can be compared with the girl next door.

"The girl next door would be too tall if an inch were added to her height, and too short if an inch were taken away. Another grain of powder would make her too pale; another touch of rouge would make her too red. Her eye-

7

brows are like the plumage of the kingfisher, her flesh is like snow. Her waist is like a roll of new silk, her teeth are like little shells. A single one of her smiles would perturb the whole city of Yang and derange the suburb of Hsia-ts'ai.[1] For three years this lady has been climbing the garden wall and peeping at me, yet I have never succumbed.

"How different is the behaviour of master Tēng-t'u! His wife has a woolly head and misshapen ears; projecting teeth irregularly set; a crook in her back and a halt in her gait. Moreover, she has running sores in front and behind.

"Yet Tēng-t'u fell in love with her and caused her to bear him five children.

"I would have your Majesty consider which of us is the debauchee."

Sung Yü was not dismissed from court.

[1] Fashionable quarters in the capital of Ch'u state.

8

The Great Summons

When Ch'ü Yüan (fourth century B.C.) had been exiled from the Court for nine years, he became so despondent that he feared his soul would part from his body and he would die. It was then that he made the poem called "The Great Summons", calling upon his soul not to leave him.

Green Spring receiveth
The vacant earth;
The white sun shineth;
Spring wind provoketh
To burst and burgeon
Each sprout and flower.
In those dark caves where Winter lurketh
Hide not, my Soul!
O Soul come back again! O, do not stray!

O Soul come back again and go not east or west,
or north or south!
For to the East a mighty water drowneth Earth's
other shore;
Tossed on its waves and heaving with its tides
The hornless Dragon of the Ocean rideth:
Clouds gather low and fogs enfold the sea
And gleaming ice drifts past.
O Soul go not to the East,
To the silent Valley of Sunrise!

9

O Soul go not to the South
Where mile on mile the earth is burnt away
And poisonous serpents slither through the flames;
Where on precipitous paths or in deep woods
Tigers and leopards prowl,
And water-scorpions wait;
Where the king-python rears his giant head.
O Soul, go not to the South
Where the three-footed tortoise spits disease!

O Soul go not to the West
Where level wastes of sand stretch on and on;
And demons rage, swine-headed, hairy-skinned,
With bulging eyes;
Who in wild laughter gnash projecting fangs.
O Soul go not to the West
Where many perils wait!

O Soul go not to the North,
To the Lame Dragon's frozen peaks;
Where trees and grasses dare not grow;
Where a river runs too wide to cross
And too deep to plumb,
And the sky is white with snow
And the cold cuts and kills.
O Soul seek not to fill
The treacherous voids of the North!

O Soul come back to idleness and peace.
In quietude enjoy
The lands of Ching and Ch'u.
There work your will and follow your desire
Till sorrow is forgot,
And carelessness shall bring you length of days.
O Soul come back to joys beyond all telling!

Where thirty cubits high at harvest-time
The corn is stacked;
Where pies are cooked of millet and bearded-maize.
Guests watch the steaming bowls
And sniff the pungency of peppered herbs.
The cunning cook adds slices of bird-flesh,
Pigeon and yellow-heron and black-crane.
They taste the badger-stew.
O Soul come back to feed on foods you love!

Next are brought
Fresh turtle, and sweet chicken cooked in cheese
Pressed by the men of Ch'u.
And pickled sucking-pig
And flesh of whelps floating in liver-sauce
With salad of minced radishes in brine;
All served with that hot spice of southernwood
The land of Wu supplies.
O Soul come back to choose the meats you love!

Roasted daw, steamed widgeon and grilled quail—
On every fowl they fare.
Boiled perch and sparrow broth,—in each preserved
The separate flavour that is most its own.
O Soul come back to where such dainties wait!

The four strong liquors are warming at the fire
So that they grate not on the drinker's throat.
How fragrant rise their fumes, how cool their taste!
Such drink is not for louts or serving-men!
And wise distillers from the land of Wu
Blend unfermented spirit with white yeast
And brew the li of Ch'u.
O Soul come back and let your yearnings cease!

Reed-organs from the lands of T'ai and Ch'in
And Wei and Chēng
Gladden the feasters, and old songs are sung:
The "Rider's Song" that once
Fu-hsi, the ancient monarch, made;
And the harp-songs of Ch'u.
Then after prelude from the flutes of Chao
The ballad-singer's voice rises alone.
O Soul come back to the hollow mulberry-tree![1]

Eight and eight the dancers sway,
Weaving their steps to the poet's voice

[1] The harp.

12

Who speaks his odes and rhapsodies;
They tap their bells and beat their chimes
Rigidly, lest harp and flute
Should mar the measure.
Then rival singers of the Four Domains
Compete in melody, till not a tune
Is left unsung that human voice could sing.
O Soul come back and listen to their songs!

Then women enter whose red lips and dazzling teeth
Seduce the eye;
But meek and virtuous, trained in every art;
Fit sharers of play-time,
So soft their flesh and delicate their bones.
O Soul come back and let them ease your woe!

Then enter other ladies with laughing lips
And sidelong glances under moth-eye brows;
Whose cheeks are fresh and red;
Ladies both great of heart and long of limb,
Whose beauty by sobriety is matched.
Well-padded cheeks and ears with curving rim,
High-arching eyebrows, as with compass drawn,
Great hearts and loving gestures—all are there;
Small waists and necks as slender as the clasp
Of courtiers' brooches.
O Soul come back to those whose tenderness
Drives angry thoughts away!

Last enter those
Whose every action is contrived to please;
Black-painted eyebrows and white-powdered cheeks.
They reek with scent; with their long sleeves they brush
The faces of the feasters whom they pass,
Or pluck the coats of those who will not stay.
O Soul come back to pleasures of the night!

A summer-house with spacious rooms
And a high hall with beams stained red;
A little closet in the southern wing
Reached by a private stair.
And round the house a covered way should run
Where horses might be trained.
And sometimes riding, sometimes going afoot
You shall explore, O Soul, the parks of spring;
Your jewelled axles gleaming in the sun
And yoke inlaid with gold;
Or amid orchises and sandal-trees
Shall walk in the dark woods.
O Soul come back and live for these delights!

Peacocks shall fill your gardens; you shall rear
The roc and phœnix, and red jungle-fowl,
Whose cry at dawn assembles river storks
To join the play of cranes and ibises;
Where the wild-swan all day

Pursues the glint of idle king-fishers.
O Soul come back to watch the birds in flight!

He who has found such manifold delights
Shall feel his cheeks aglow
And the blood-spirit dancing through his limbs.
Stay with me, Soul, and share
The span of days that happiness will bring;
See sons and grandsons serving at the Court
Ennobled and enriched.
O Soul come back and bring prosperity
To house and stock!

The roads that lead to Ch'u
Shall teem with travellers as thick as clouds,
A thousand miles away.
For the Five Orders of Nobility
Shall summon sages to assist the King
And with godlike discrimination choose
The wise in council; by their aid to probe
The hidden discontents of humble men
And help the lonely poor.
O Soul come back and end what we began!

Fields, villages and lanes
Shall throng with happy men;
Good rule protect the people and make known

The King's benevolence to all the land;
Stern discipline prepare
Their natures for the soft caress of Art.
O Soul come back to where the good are praised!

Like the sun shining over the four seas
Shall be the reputation of our King;
His deeds, matched only in Heaven, shall repair
The wrongs endured by every tribe of men,—
Northward to Yu and southward to Annam,
To the Sheep's Gut Mountain and the Eastern Seas.
O Soul come back to where the wise are sought!

Behold the glorious virtues of our King
Triumphant, terrible;
Behold with solemn faces in the Hall
The Three Grand Ministers walk up and down,—
None chosen for the post save landed-lords
Or, in default, Knights of the Nine Degrees.
At the first ray of dawn already is hung
The shooting-target, where with bow in hand
And arrows under arm,
Each archer does obeisance to each,
Willing to yield his rights of precedence.
O Soul come back to where men honour still
The name of the Three Kings.[1]

[1] Yü, T'ang and Wēn, the three just rulers of antiquity.

16

Cock-Crow Song

Anonymous (first century B. C.)

In the eastern quarter dawn breaks, the stars flicker pale.
The morning cock at Ju-nan mounts the wall and crows.
The songs are over, the clock[1] run down, but still the
    feast is set.
The moon grows dim and the stars are few; morning has
    come to the world.
At a thousand gates and ten thousand doors the fish-shaped
    keys turn;
Round the Palace and up by the Castle, the crows and
    magpies are flying.

[1] A water-clock.

Lament of Hsi-chün

About the year 110 B.C. a Chinese Princess named Hsi-chün was sent, for political reasons, to be the wife of a central Asian nomad king, K'un Mo, king of the Wu-sun. When she got there, she found her husband old and decrepit. He only saw her once or twice a year, when they drank a cup of wine together. They could not converse, as they had no language in common.

My people have married me
In a far corner of Earth:
Sent me away to a strange land,
To the king of the Wu-sun.
A tent is my house,
Of felt are my walls;
Raw flesh my food
With mare's milk to drink.
Always thinking of my own country,
My heart sad within.
Would I were a yellow stork
And could fly to my old home!

18

The Orphan

Anonymous (first century B.C.)

To be an orphan,
To be fated to be an orphan,
How bitter is this lot!
When my father and mother were alive
I used to ride in a carriage
With four fine horses.
But when they both died,
My brother and sister-in-law
Sent me out to be a merchant.
In the south I travelled to the "Nine Rivers"
And in the east as far as Ch'i and Lu.
At the end of the year when I came home
I dared not tell them what I had suffered—
Of the lice and vermin in my head,
Of the dust in my face and eyes.
My brother told me to get ready the dinner,
My sister-in-law told me to see after the horses.
I was always going up into the hall
And running down again to the parlour.
My tears fell like rain.

In the morning they sent me to draw water,
I didn't get back till night-fall.
My hands were all sore
And I had no shoes.
I walked the cold earth
Treading on thorns and brambles.
As I stopped to pull out the thorns,
How bitter my heart was!
My tears fell and fell
And I went on sobbing and sobbing.
In winter I have no great-coat;
Nor in summer, thin clothes.
It is no pleasure to be alive.
I had rather quickly leave the earth
And go beneath the Yellow Springs.[1]
The April winds blow
And the grass is growing green.
In the third month—silkworms and mulberries,
In the sixth month—the melon-harvest.
I went out with the melon-cart
And just as I was coming home
The melon-cart turned over.
The people who came to help me were few,
But the people who ate the melons were many,
All they left me was the stalks—
To take home as fast as I could.
My brother and sister-in-law were harsh,

[1] Hades.

20

They asked me all sorts of awful questions.
Why does everyone in the village hate me?
I want to write a letter and send it
To my mother and father under the earth,
And tell them I can't go on any longer
Living with my brother and sister-in-law.

The Sick Wife

She had been ill for years and years;
She sent for me to say something.
She couldn't say what she wanted
Because of the tears that kept coming of themselves.
"I have burdened you with orphan children,
With orphan children two or three.
Don't let our children go hungry or cold;
If they do wrong, don't slap or beat them.
When you take out the baby, rock it in your arms.
Don't forget to do that."
Last she said,
"When I carried them in my arms they had no clothes
And now their jackets have no linings."   [*She dies.*

I shut the doors and barred the windows
And left the motherless children.
When I got to the market and met my friends, I wept.
I sat down and could not go with them.
I asked them to buy some cakes for my children.
In the presence of my friends I sobbed and cried.
I tried not to grieve, but sorrow would not cease.
I felt in my pocket and gave my friends some money.
When I got home I found my children

Calling to be taken into their mother's arms.
I walked up and down in the empty room
This way and that a long while.
Then I went away from it and said to myself,
"I will forget and never speak of her again."

Meeting in the Road

In a narrow road where there was not room to pass
My carriage met the carriage of a young man.
And while his axle was touching my axle
In the narrow road I asked him where he lived.
"The place where I live is easy enough to find,
Easy to find and difficult to forget.
The gates of my house are built of yellow gold,
The hall of my house is paved with white jade,
On the hall table flagons of wine are set,
I had summoned to serve me dancers of Han-tan.[1]
In the midst of a courtyard grows a cassia-tree,—
And candles on its branches flaring away in the night."

[1] Capital of the kingdom of Chao, where the people were famous for their beauty.

"Old Poem"

At fifteen I went with the army,
At fourscore I came home.
On the way I met a man from the village,
I asked him who there was at home.
"That over there is your house,
All covered over with trees and bushes."
Rabbits had run in at the dog-hole,
Pheasants flew down from the beams of the roof.
In the courtyard was growing some wild grain;
And by the well, some wild mallows.
I'll boil the grain and make porridge,
I'll pluck the mallows and make soup.
Soup and porridge are both cooked,
But there is no one to eat them with.
I went out and looked towards the east,
While tears fell and wetted my clothes.

The Golden Palace

Anonymous (first century B. C.)

We go to the Golden Palace:
We set out the jade cups.
We summon the honoured guests
To enter at the Golden Gate.
They enter at the Golden Gate
And go to the Golden Hall.
In the Eastern Kitchen the meat is sliced and ready—
Roast beef and boiled pork and mutton.
The Master of the Feast hands round the wine.
The harp-players sound their clear chords.

The cups are pushed aside and we face each other at chess:
The rival pawns are marshalled rank against rank.
The fire glows and the smoke puffs and curls;
From the incense-burner rises a delicate fragrance.
The clear wine has made our cheeks red;
Round the table joy and peace prevail.
May those who shared in this day's delight
Through countless autumns enjoy like felicity.

Fighting South of the Castle

Anonymous (circa 124 B. C.)

They fought south of the Castle,
They died north of the wall.
They died in the moors and were not buried.
Their flesh was the food of crows.
"Tell the crows we are not afraid;
We have died in the moors and cannot be buried.
Crows, how can our bodies escape you?"
The waters flowed deep
And the rushes in the pool were dark.
The riders fought and were slain:
Their horses wander neighing.
By the bridge there was a house.[1]
Was it south, was it north?
The harvest was never gathered.
How can we give you your offerings?
You served your Prince faithfully,
Though all in vain.
I think of you, faithful soldiers;
Your service shall not be forgotten.
For in the morning you went out to battle
And at night you did not return.

[1] There is no trace of it left. This passage describes the havoc of war. The harvest has not been gathered: therefore corn-offerings cannot be made to the spirits of the dead.

The Eastern Gate

Anonymous (first century B. C.)

A poor man determines to go out into the world and make his fortune. His wife tries to detain him.

I went out at the eastern gate:
I never thought to return.
But I came back to the gate with my heart full of sorrow.

There was not a peck of rice in the bin:
There was not a coat hanging on the pegs.
So I took my sword and went towards the gate.
My wife and child clutched at my coat and wept:
"Some people want to be rich and grand:
I only want to share my porridge with you.
Above, we have the blue waves of the sky:
Below, the yellow face of this little child."
    "Dear wife, I cannot stay.
    Soon it will be too late.
    When one is growing old
    One cannot put things off."

Old and New

Anonymous (*first century* B. C.)

She went up the mountain to pluck wild herbs;
She came down the mountain and met her former husband.
She knelt down and asked her former husband
"What do you find your new wife like?"
"My new wife, although her talk is clever,
Cannot charm me as my old wife could.
In beauty of face there is not much to choose,
But in usefulness they are not at all alike.
My new wife comes in from the road to meet me;
My old wife always came down from her tower.
My new wife is clever at embroidering silk;
My old wife was good at plain sewing.
Of silk embroidery one can do an inch a day;
Of plain sewing, more than five feet.
Putting her silks by the side of your sewing,
I see that the new will not compare with the old."

South of the Great Sea

My love is living
To the south of the Great Sea.
What shall I send to greet him?
Two pearls and a comb of tortoise-shell:
I'll send them to him packed in a box of jade.
They tell me he is not true:
They tell me he dashed my box to the ground,
Dashed it to the ground and burnt it
And scattered its ashes to the wind.
From this day to the ends of time
I must never think of him,
Never again think of him.
The cocks are crowing,
And the dogs are barking—
My brother and his wife will soon know.[1]
The autumn wind is blowing;
The morning wind is sighing.
In a moment the sun will rise in the east
And then *it* too will know.

[1] *I.e.*, about her engagement being broken off.

The Other Side of the Valley

I am a prisoner in the hands of the enemy,
Enduring the shame of captivity.
My bones stick out and my strength is gone
Through not getting enough to eat.
My brother is a Mandarin
And his horses are fed on maize.
Why can't he spare a little money
To send and ransom me?

Oaths of Friendship

In the country of Yüeh when a man made friends with another they set up an altar of earth and sacrificed upon it a dog and a cock, reciting this oath as they did so:

If you were riding in a coach
And I were wearing a "li",[1]
And one day we met in the road,
You would get down and bow.
If you were carrying a "tēng",[2]
And I were riding on a horse,
And one day we met in the road
I would get down for you.

Shang Ya!
I want to be your friend
For ever and ever without break or decay.
When the hills are all flat
And the rivers are all dry,
When it lightens and thunders in winter,
When it rains and snows in summer,
When Heaven and Earth mingle—
Not till then will I part from you.

[1] A peasant's coat made of straw.
[2] An umbrella under which a cheap-jack sells his wares.

32

Burial Songs

[1]

"The Dew on the Garlic-leaf"
Sung at the burial of kings and princes.

How swiftly it dries,
The dew on the garlic-leaf.
The dew that dries so fast
To-morrow will fall again.
But he whom we carry to the grave
Will never more return.

[2]

"The Graveyard"
Sung at the burial of common men.

What man's land is the graveyard?
It is the crowded home of ghosts,—
Wise and foolish shoulder to shoulder.
The King of the Dead claims them all;
Man's fate knows no tarrying.

Five "Tzŭ-yeh" Songs

[1]

At the time when blossoms
Fall from the cherry-tree:
On a day when yellow birds
Hovered in the branches—
You said you must stop,
Because your horse was tired:
I said I must go,
Because my silkworms were hungry.

[2]

All night I could not sleep
Because of the moonlight on my bed.
I kept on hearing a voice calling:
Out of Nowhere, Nothing answered "yes".

[3]

I will carry my coat and not put on my belt;
With unpainted eyebrows I will stand at the
    front window.
My tiresome petticoat keeps on flapping about;
If it opens a little, I shall blame the spring wind.

[4]

I heard my love was going to Yang-chou
And went with him as far as Ch'u-shan.
For a moment when you held me fast in your
    outstretched arms
I thought the river stood still and did not flow.

[5]

I have brought my pillow and am lying at the
    northern window,
So come to me and play with me awhile.
With so much quarrelling and so few kisses
How long do you think our love can last?

The Autumn Wind

By Wu-ti (157-87 B. C.), sixth emperor of the Han dynasty.
He came to the throne when he was only sixteen. In this poem he regrets that he is obliged to go on an official journey, leaving his mistress
behind in the capital. He is seated in his state barge surrounded by his
ministers.

Autumn wind rises: white clouds fly.
Grass and trees wither: geese go south.
Orchids all in bloom: chrysanthemums smell sweet.
I think of my lovely lady: I never can forget.
Floating-pagoda boat crosses Fēn River.
Across the mid-stream white waves rise;
Flute and drum keep time to sound of the rowers' song;
Amidst revel and feasting, sad thoughts come;
Youth's years how few! Age how sure!

Seventeen Old Poems

The following seventeen poems are from a series known as the Nineteen Pieces of Old Poetry. Some have been attributed to Mei Shēng (first century B. C.), and one to Fu I (first century A. D.). They are manifestly not all by the same hand nor of the same date. Internal evidence shows that No. 3 at least was written after the date of Mei Shēng's death. These poems had an enormous influence on all subsequent poetry, and many of the habitual clichés of Chinese verse are taken from them. I have omitted two because of their marked inferiority.

[1]

On and on, always on and on
Away from you, parted by a life-parting.[1]
Going from one another ten thousand "li",
Each in a different corner of the World.
The way between is difficult and long,
Face to face how shall we meet again?
The Tartar horse prefers the North wind,
The bird from Yüeh nests on the Southern branch.
Since we parted the time is already long,
Daily my clothes hang looser round my waist.
Floating clouds obscure the white sun,
The wandering one has quite forgotten home.

[1] The opposite of a parting by death.

Thinking of you has made me suddenly old,
The months and years swiftly draw to their close.
I'll put you out of my mind and forget for ever
And try with all my might to eat and thrive.[1]

[2]

Green, green,
The grass by the river-bank.
Thick, thick,
The willow trees in the garden.
Sad, sad,
The lady in the tower.
White, white,
Sitting at the casement window.
Fair, fair,
Her red-powdered face.
Small, small,
She puts out her pale hand.
Once she was a dancing-house girl,
Now she is a wandering man's wife.
The wandering man went, but did not return.
It is hard alone to keep an empty bed.

[1] The popular, but erroneous, interpretation of these two lines is:

"That I'm cast away and rejected I will not repine,
But only hope with all my heart you're well."

38

[3]

Green, green,
The cypress on the mound.
Firm, firm,
The boulder in the stream.
Man's life lived within this world,
Is like the sojourning of a hurried traveller.
A cup of wine together will make us glad,
And a little friendship is no little matter.

Yoking my chariot I urge my stubborn horses.
I wander about in the streets of Wan and Lo.
In Lo Town how fine everything is!
The "Caps and Belts"[1] go seeking each other out.
The great boulevards are intersected by lanes,
Wherein are the town-houses of Royal Dukes
The two palaces stare at each other from afar,
The twin gates rise a hundred feet.
By prolonging the feast let us keep our hearts gay,
And leave no room for sadness to creep in.

[1] High officers.

[4]

Of this day's glorious feast and revel
The pleasure and delight are difficult to describe.
Plucking the lute they sent forth lingering sounds,
The new melodies in beauty reached the divine.
Skilful singers intoned the high words,
Those who knew the tune heard the trueness of their singing.
We sat there each with the same desire
And like thoughts by each unexpressed:
"Man in the world lodging for a single life-time
Passes suddenly like dust borne on the wind.
Then let us hurry out with high steps
And be the first to reach the highways and fords:
Rather than stay at home wretched and poor
For long years plunged in sordid grief."

[5]

In the north-west there is a high house,
Its top level with the floating clouds.
Embroidered curtains thinly screen its windows,
Its storied tower is built on three steps.
From above there comes a noise of playing and singing,
The tune sounding, oh! how sad!
Who can it be, playing so sad a tune?
Surely it must be Ch'i Liang's[1] wife.

[1] Who had no father, no husband, and no children.

40

The tranquil "D" follows the wind's rising,
The middle lay lingers indecisive.
To each note, two or three sobs,
Her high will conquered by overwhelming grief.
She does not regret that she is left so sad,
But minds that so few can understand her song.
She wants to become those two wild geese
That with beating wings rise high aloft.

[6]

Crossing the river I pluck hibiscus-flowers:
In the orchid-swamps are many fragrant herbs.
I gather them, but who shall I send them to?
My love is living in lands far away.
I turn and look towards my own country:
The long road stretches on for ever.
The same heart, yet a different dwelling:
Always fretting, till we are grown old!

[7]

A bright moon illumines the night-prospect:
The house-cricket chirrups on the eastern wall.
The Handle of the Pole-star points to the Beginning
    of Winter.
The host of stars is scattered over the sky.
The white dew wets the moor-grasses,—

41

With sudden swiftness the times and seasons change.
The autumn cicada sings among the trees,
The swallows, alas, whither are they gone?

Once I had a same-house friend,
He took flight and rose high away.
He did not remember how once we went hand in hand,
But left me like footsteps behind one in the dust.

In the South is the Winnowing-fan and the Pole-star
    in the North,
And a Herd-boy[1] whose ox has never borne the yoke.
A friend who is not firm as a great rock
Is of no profit and idly bears the name.

[8]

In the courtyard there grows a strange tree,
Its green leaves ooze with a fragrant moisture.
Holding the branch I cut a flower from the tree,
Meaning to send it away to the person I love.
Its sweet smell fills my sleeves and lap.
The road is long, how shall I get it there?
Such a thing is not fine enough to send:
But it may remind him of the time that has past since he left.[2]

[1] Name of a star. The Herd-boy, who is only figuratively speaking a herd-boy, is like the friend who is no real friend.
[2] I.e. (supposing he went away in the autumn), remind him that spring has come.

42

[9]

Far away twinkles the Herd-boy star;
Brightly shines the Lady of the Han River.
Slender, slender she plies her white fingers.
Click, click go the wheels of her spinning-loom.
At the end of the day she has not finished her task;
Her bitter tears fall like streaming rain.
The Han River runs shallow and clear;
Set between them, how short a space!
But the river water will not let them pass,
Gazing at each other but never able to speak.

[10]

Turning my chariot I yoke my horses and go.
On and on down the long roads
The autumn winds shake the hundred grasses.
On every side, how desolate and bare!
The things I meet are all new things,
Their strangeness hastens the coming of old age.
Prosperity and decay each have their season.
Success is bitter when it is slow in coming.
Man's life is not metal or stone,
He cannot far prolong the days of his fate.
Suddenly he follows in the way of things that change.
Fame is the only treasure that endures.

The Eastern Castle stands tall and high;
Far and wide stretch the towers that guard it.
The whirling wind uprises and shakes the earth;
The autumn grasses grow thick and green.
The four seasons alternate without pause,
The year's end hurries swiftly on.
The Bird of the Morning Wind is stricken with sorrow,
The frail cicada suffers and is hard pressed.
Free and clear, let us loosen the bonds of our hearts.
Why should we go on always restraining and binding?
In Yen and Chao are many fair ladies,
Beautiful people with faces like jade.
Their clothes are made all of silk gauze,
They stand at the door practising tranquil lays.
The echo of their singing, how sad it sounds!
By the pitch of the song one knows the stops have
    been tightened.
To ease their minds they arrange their shawls and belts;
Lowering their song, a little while they pause.
"I should like to be those two flying swallows
Who are carrying clay to nest in the eaves of your house."

[12]

I drive my chariot up to the Eastern Gate;
From afar I see the graveyard north of the Wall.
The white aspens how they murmur, murmur;
Pines and cypresses flank the broad paths.
Beneath lie men who died long ago;
Black, black is the long night that holds them.
Deep down beneath the Yellow Springs,
Thousands of years they lie without waking.

In infinite succession light and darkness shift,
And years vanish like the morning dew.
Man's life is like a sojourning,
His longevity lacks the firmness of stone and metal.
For ever it has been that mourners in their turn
        were mourned,
Saint and Sage,—all alike are trapped.
Seeking by food to obtain Immortality
Many have been the dupe of strange drugs.
Better far to drink good wine
And clothe our bodies in robes of satin and silk.

13

The dead are gone and with them we cannot converse.
The living are here and ought to have our love.
Leaving the city-gate I look ahead
And see before me only mounds and tombs.
The old graves are ploughed up into fields,
The pines and cypresses are hewn for timber.
In the white aspens sad winds sing;
Their long murmuring kills my heart with grief.
I want to go home, to ride to my village-gate.
I want to go back, but there's no road back.

14

The years of a lifetime do not reach a hundred,
Yet they contain a thousand years' sorrow.
When days are short and the dull nights long,
Why not take a lamp and wander forth?
If you want to be happy you must do it now,
There is no waiting till an after-time.
The fool who's loath to spend the wealth he's got
Becomes the laughing-stock of after ages.
It is true that Master Wang became immortal,
But how can *we* hope to share his lot?

[15]

Cold, cold the year draws to its end,
The crickets and grasshoppers make a doleful chirping.
The chill wind increases its violence.
My wandering love has no coat to cover him.
He gave his embroidered furs to the Lady of Lo,
But from me his bedfellow he is quite estranged.
Sleeping alone in the depth of the long night
In a dream I thought I saw the light of his face.
My dear one thought of our old joys together,
He came in his chariot and gave me the front reins.
I wanted so to prolong our play and laughter,
To hold his hand and go back with him in his coach.
But, when he had come he would not stay long
Nor stop to go with me to the Inner Chamber.
Truly without the falcon's wings to carry me
How can I rival the flying wind's swiftness?
I go and lean at the gate and think of my grief,
My falling tears wet the double gates.

[16]

At the beginning of winter a cold spirit comes,
The North Wind blows—chill, chill.
My sorrows being many, I know the length of the nights,
Raising my head I look at the stars in their places.

47

On the fifteenth day the bright moon is full,
On the twentieth day the "toad and hare" wane.[1]
A stranger came to me from a distant land
And brought me a single scroll with writing on it;
At the top of the scroll was written "Do not forget",
At the bottom was written "Goodbye for Ever".
I put the letter away in the folds of my dress,
For three years the writing did not fade.
How with an undivided heart I loved you
I fear that you will never know or guess.

[17]

The bright moon, oh, how white it shines,
Shines down on the gauze curtains of my bed.
Racked by sorrow I toss and cannot sleep.
Picking up my clothes, I wander up and down.
My absent love says that he is happy,
But I would rather he said he was coming back.
Out in the courtyard I stand hesitating, alone.
To whom can I tell the sad thoughts I think?
Staring before me I enter my room again;
Falling tears wet my mantle and robe.

[1] The "toad and hare" correspond to our "man in the moon". The waning
of the moon symbolizes the waning of the lover's affection.

48

Li Fu-jēn

By Wu-ti

The sound of her silk skirt has stopped.
On the marble pavement dust grows.
Her empty room is cold and still.
Fallen leaves are piled against the doors.
    Longing for that lovely lady
How can I bring my aching heart to rest?

The above poem was written by Wu-ti when his mistress, Li Fu-jēn, died. Unable to bear his grief, he sent for wizards from all parts of China, hoping that they would be able to put him into communication with her spirit. At last one of them managed to project her shape on to a curtain. The emperor cried:

> *Is it or isn't it?*
> *I stand and look.*
> *The swish, swish of a silk skirt.*
> *How slow she comes!*

Song of Snow-White Heads

By Cho Wên-chün

Ssŭ-ma Hsiang-ju (died 118 B. C.) was a young poet who had lost his position at court owing to ill-health. One day Cho Wên-chün, a rich man's daughter, heard him singing at a feast given by her father. She eloped with him that night, and they set up a wine-shop together. After a time Hsiang-ju became famous as a poet, but his character was marred by love of money. He sold love-poems, which the ladies of the palace sent to the emperor in order to win his favour. Finally, he gave presents to the "ladies of Mo-ling", hoping to secure a concubine. It was this step that induced his mistress, Cho Wên-chün, to write the following poem.

Our love was pure
As the snow on the mountains:
White as a moon
Between the clouds—
They're telling me
Your thoughts are double;
That's why I've come
To break it off.
To-day we'll drink
A cup of wine.
To-morrow we'll part
Beside the Canal:

50

Walking about,
Beside the Canal,
Where its branches divide
East and west.
Alas and alas,
And again alas.
So must a girl
Cry when she's married,
If she find not a man
Of single heart,
Who will not leave her
Till her hair is white.

To His Wife

By General Su Wu? (circa 100 B. C.)

Since our hair was plaited and we became man and wife
The love between us was never broken by doubt.
So let us be merry this night together,
Feasting and playing while the good time lasts.

I suddenly remember the distance that I must travel;
I spring from bed and look out to see the time.
The stars and planets are all grown dim in the sky;
Long, long is the road; I cannot stay.
I am going on service, away to the battle-ground,
And I do not know when I shall come back.
I hold your hand with only a deep sigh;
Afterwards, tears—in the days when we are parted.
With all your might enjoy the spring flowers,
But do not forget the time of our love and pride.
Know that if I live, I will come back again,
And if I die, we will go on thinking of each other.

Li Ling

[Parting from Su Wu]

(Authorship Uncertain)

The good time will never come back again:
In a moment,—our parting will be over.
Anxiously—we halt at the road-side,
Hesitating—we embrace where the fields begin.
The clouds above are floating across the sky:
Swiftly, swiftly passing: or blending together.
The waves in the wind lose their fixed place
And are rolled away each to a corner of Heaven.
From now onwards—long must be our parting,
So let us stop again for a little while.
I wish I could ride on the wings of the morning wind
And go with you right to your journey's end.

*Li Ling and Su Wu were both prisoners in the land of the Huns.
After nineteen years Su Wu was released. Li Ling would not go back
with him. When invited to do so, he got up and danced, singing:*

I came ten thousand leagues
Across sandy deserts

In the service of my Prince,
To break the Hun tribes.
My way was blocked and barred,
My arrows and sword broken.
My armies had faded away,
My reputation had gone.

My old mother is long dead.
Although I want to requite my Prince
        How can I return?

Ch'in Chia

Ch'in Chia (*first century A. D.*) *was summoned to take up an* *appointment at the capital at a time when his wife was ill and staying* *with her parents. He was therefore unable to say goodbye to her, and* *sent her three poems instead. This is the last of the three.*

Solemn, solemn the coachman gets ready to go:
"Chiang, chiang" the harness bells ring.
At break of dawn I must start on my long journey:
At cock-crow I must gird on my belt.
I turn back and look at the empty room:
For a moment I almost think I see you there.
One parting, but ten thousand regrets:
As I take my seat, my heart is unquiet.
What shall I do to tell you all my thoughts?
How can I let you know of all my love?
Precious hairpins make the head to shine
And bright mirrors can reflect beauty.
Fragrant herbs banish evil smells
And the scholar's harp has a clear note.
The man in the Book of Odes[1] who was given a quince
Wanted to pay it back with diamonds and rubies.
When I think of all the things you have done for me,
How ashamed I am to have done so little for you!
Although I know that it is a poor return,
All I can give you is this description of my feelings.

[1] Odes, v, 10.

Ch'in Chia's Wife's Reply

My poor body is alas unworthy:
I was ill when first you brought me home.
Limp and weary in the house—
Time passed and I got no better.
We could hardly ever see each other:
I could not serve you as I ought.
Then you received the Imperial Mandate:
You were ordered to go far away to the City.
Long, long must be our parting:
I was not destined to tell you my thoughts.
I stood on tiptoe gazing into the distance,
Interminably gazing at the road that had taken you.
With thoughts of you my mind is obsessed:
In my dreams I see the light of your face.
Now you are started on your long journey
Each day brings you further from me.
Oh that I had a bird's wings
And high flying could follow you.
Long I sob and long I cry:
The tears fall down and wet my skirt.

Song

By Sung Tzŭ-hou (second century A.D.)

On the Eastern Way at the city of Lo-yang
At the edge of the road peach-trees and plum-trees grow;
On the two sides,—flower matched by flower;
Across the road,—leaf touching leaf.

A spring wind rises from the north-east;
Flowers and leaves gently nod and sway.
Up the road somebody's daughter comes
Carrying a basket, to gather silkworms' food.

[She sees the fruit trees in blossom and, forgetting about
her silkworms, begins to pluck the branches.]

With her slender hand she breaks a branch from the tree;
The flowers fall, tossed and scattered in the wind.

The tree says:
"Lovely lady, I never did you harm;
Why should you hate me and do me injury?"

The lady answers:

"At high autumn in the eighth and ninth moons
When the white dew changes to hoar-frost,
At the year's end the wind would have lashed your boughs,
Your sweet fragrance could not have lasted long.
Though in the autumn your leaves patter to the ground,
When spring comes, your gay bloom returns.
But in men's lives when their bright youth is spent
Joy and love never come back again."

Satire on Paying Calls in August

By Ch'êng Hsiao (circa A. D. 250)

When I was young, throughout the hot season
There were no carriages driving about the roads,
People shut their doors and lay down in the cool:
Or if they went out, it was not to pay calls.
Nowadays—ill-bred, ignorant fellows,
When they feel the heat, make for a friend's house.
The unfortunate host, when he hears someone coming
Scowls and frowns, but can think of no escape.
"There's nothing for it but to rise and go to the door,"
And in his comfortable seat he groans and sighs.

The conversation does not end quickly:
Prattling and babbling, what a lot he says!
Only when one is almost dead with fatigue
He asks at last if one isn't finding him tiring.
[One's arm is almost in half with continual fanning:
The sweat is pouring down one's neck in streams.]
Do not say that this is a small matter:
I consider the practice a blot on our social life.
I therefore caution all wise men
That August visitors should not be admitted.

On the Death of His Father

By Wei Wēn-ti, son of Ts'ao Ts'ao, who founded the dynasty
of Wei, and died in A. D. 220. (The poem has been wrongly
attributed to Han Wēn-ti, died 157 B. C.)

I look up and see / his curtains and bed:
I look down and examine / his table and mat.
The things are there / just as before.
But the man they belonged to / is not there.
His spirit suddenly / has taken flight
And left me behind / far away.
To whom shall I look, / on whom rely?
My tears flow / in an endless stream.
"Yu, yu" / cry the wandering deer
As they carry fodder / to their young in the wood.
Flap, flap / fly the birds
As they carry their little ones / back to the nest.
I alone / am desolate
Dreading the days / of our long parting:
My grieving heart's / settled pain
No one else / can understand.
There is a saying / among people
"Sorrow makes us / grow old".

Alas, alas / for my white hairs!
All too early / they have come!
Long wailing, / long sighing
My thoughts are fixed on my sage parent.
They say the good / live long:
Then why was *he* / not spared?

The Campaign Against Wu

Two Poems by Wei Wên-ti (A. D. 188-227)

[1]

My charioteer hastens to yoke my carriage,
For I must go on a journey far away.
"Where are you going on your journey far away?"
To the land of Wu where my enemies are.
But I must ride many thousand miles,
Beyond the Eastern Road that leads to Wu.
Between the rivers bitter winds blow,
Swiftly flow the waters of Huai and Ssŭ.
I want to take a skiff and cross these rivers,
But alas for me, where shall I find a boat?
To sit idle is not my desire:
Gladly enough would I go to my country's aid.

[2]

(*He abandons the campaign*)

In the North-west there is a floating cloud
Stretched on high, like a chariot's canvas-awning.
Alas that I was born in these times,
To be blown along like a cloud puffed by the wind!
It has blown me away far to the South-east,
On and on till I came to Wu-hui.
Wu-hui is not my country:
Why should I go on staying and staying here?
I will give it up and never speak of it again,—
This being abroad and always living in dread.

The Ruins of Lo-yang

By Ts'ao Chih (A. D. 192–232), third son of Ts'ao Ts'ao.
He was a great favourite with his father till he made a mistake in a
campaign. In this poem he returns to look at the ruins of Lo-yang,
where he used to live. It had been sacked by Tung Cho.

I climb to the ridge of Pei Mang Mountain
And look down on the city of Lo-yang.
In Lo-yang how still it is!
Palaces and houses all burnt to ashes.
Walls and fences all broken and gaping,
Thorns and brambles shooting up to the sky.
I do not see the old old-men:
I only see the new young men.
I turn aside, for the straight road is lost:
The fields are overgrown and will never be
        ploughed again.
I have been away such a long time
That I do not know which street is which.
How sad and ugly the empty moors are!
A thousand miles without the smoke of a chimney.
I think of the house I lived in all those years:
        I am heart-tied and cannot speak.

The preceding poem vaguely recalls a famous Anglo-Saxon
fragment which I will make intelligible by semi-translation:

"Wondrous was the wall-stone,
Weirdly[1] broken;
Burgh-steads bursten,
Giants' work tumbleth,
Roofs are wrenched,
Towers totter,
Bereft of rune-gates.
Smoke is on the plaster,
Scarred the shower-burghs,
Shorn and shattered,
By eld under-eaten.
Earth's grip haveth
Wealders[2] and workmen."

[1] By Fate.
[2] Rulers.

The Cock-Fight

By Ts'ao Chih

Our wandering eyes are sated with the dancer's skill,
Our ears are weary with the sound of "kung"
    and "shang".[1]
Our host is silent and sits doing nothing:
All the guests go on to places of amusement.

On long benches the sportsmen sit ranged
Round a cleared room, watching the fighting-cocks.
The gallant birds are all in battle-trim:
They raise their tails and flap defiantly.
Their beating wings stir the calm air:
Their angry eyes gleam with a red light.
Where their beaks have struck, the fine feathers are
    scattered:
With their strong talons they wound again and again.
Their long cries enter the blue clouds;
Their flapping wings tirelessly beat and throb.
"Pray God the lamp-oil lasts a little longer,
Then I shall not leave without winning the match!"

[1] Notes of the scale.

66

A Vision

By Ts'ao Chih

In the Nine Provinces there is not room enough:
I want to soar high among the clouds,
And, far beyond the Eight Limits of the compass,
Cast my gaze across the unmeasured void.
I will wear as my gown the red mists of sunrise,
And as my skirt the white fringes of the clouds:
My canopy—the dim lustre of Space:
My chariot—six dragons mounting heavenward:
And before the light of Time has shifted a pace
Suddenly stand upon the World's blue rim.
    The doors of Heaven swing open,
The double gates shine with a red light.
I roam and linger in the palace of Wēn-ch'ang,[1]
I climb up to the hall of T'ai-wei.[1]
The Lord God lies at his western lattice:
And the lesser Spirits are together in the eastern gallery.
They wash me in a bath of rainbow-spray
And gird me with a belt of jasper and rubies.
I wander at my ease gathering divine herbs:
I bend down and touch the scented flowers.
Wang-tzŭ[2] gives me drugs of long-life
And Hsien-mēn[2] hands me strange potions.
By the partaking of food I evade the rites of Death:
My span is extended to the enjoyment of life everlasting.

[1] Stars.   [2] Immortals.

Regret

By Yüan Chi (A.D. 210-263)

When I was young I learnt fencing
And was better at it than Crooked Castle.[1]
My spirit was high as the rolling clouds
And my fame resounded beyond the World.
I took my sword to the desert sands,
I watered my horse at the Nine Moors.
My flags and banners flapped in the wind,
And nothing was heard but the song of my drums.

War and its travels have made me sad,
And a fierce anger burns within me:
It's thinking of how I've wasted my time
That makes this fury tear my heart.

[1] A famous general.

68

The Curtain of the Wedding Bed

By Liu Hsün's wife (third century A. D.)

After she had been married to him for a long while, General Liu Hsün sent his wife back to her home, because he had fallen in love with a girl of the Ssu-ma family.

Flap, flap, you curtain in front of our bed!
I hung you there to screen us from the light of day.
I brought you with me when I left my father's house;
Now I am taking you back with me again.
I will fold you up and lay you flat in your box.
Curtain—shall I ever take you out again?

Taoist Song

By Chi K'ang (A. D. 223-262)

I will cast out Wisdom and reject Learning.
My thoughts shall wander in the Great Void (bis)
Always repenting of wrongs done
Will never bring my heart to rest.
I cast my hook in a single stream;
But my joy is as though I possessed a Kingdom.
I loose my hair and go singing;
To the four frontiers men join in my refrain.
This is the purport of my song:
"My thoughts shall wander in the Great Void."

A Gentle Wind

By Fu Hsüan (died A. D. 278)

A gentle wind fans the calm night:
A bright moon shines on the high tower.
A voice whispers, but no one answers when I call:
A shadow stirs, but no one comes when I beckon.
The kitchen-man brings in a dish of lentils:
Wine is there, but I do not fill my cup.
Contentment with poverty is Fortune's best gift:
Riches and Honour are the handmaids of Disaster.
Though gold and gems by the world are sought and prized,
To me they seem no more than weeds, or chaff.

Woman

By Fu Hsüan

How sad it is to be a woman!
Nothing on earth is held so cheap.
Boys stand leaning at the door
Like Gods fallen out of Heaven.
Their hearts brave the Four Oceans,
The wind and dust of a thousand miles.
No one is glad when a girl is born:
By *her* the family sets no store.
When she grows up, she hides in her room
Afraid to look a man in the face.
No one cries when she leaves her home—
Sudden as clouds when the rain stops.
She bows her head and composes her face,
Her teeth are pressed on her red lips:
She bows and kneels countless times.
She must humble herself even to the servants.
His love is distant as the stars in Heaven,
Yet the sunflower bends toward the sun.
Their hearts more sundered than water and fire—
A hundred evils are heaped upon her.

72

Her face will follow the years' changes:
Her lord will find new pleasures.
They that were once like substance and shadow
Are now as far as Hu from Ch'in.[1]
Yet Hu and Ch'in shall sooner meet
Than they whose parting is like Ts'an and Ch'ēn.[2]

[1] Two lands.
[2] Two stars.

Day Dreams

By Tso Ssŭ (third century A. D.)

When I was young I played with a soft brush
And was passionately devoted to reading all sorts of books.
In prose I made Chia I my standard:
In verse I imitated Ssŭ-ma Hsiang-ju.
But then the arrows began singing at the frontier.
And a winged summons came flying to the City.
Although arms were not my profession,
I had once read Jang-chü's war-book.
I shouted aloud and my cries rent the air:
I felt as though Tung Wu were already annihilated.
The scholar's knife cuts best at its first use
And my dreams hurried on to the completion of my plan.
I wanted at a stroke to clear the Yang-tze and Hsiang,
At a glance to quell the Tibetans and Hu.
When my task was done, I should not accept a barony,
But refusing with a bow, retire to a cottage in the country.

The Scholar in the Narrow Street

By Tso Ssŭ

Flap, flap, the captive bird in the cage
Beating its wings against the four corners.
Depressed, depressed the scholar in the narrow street:
Clasping a shadow, he dwells in an empty house.
When he goes out, there is nowhere for him to go:
Bunches and brambles block up his path.
He composes a memorial, but it is rejected and unread,
He is left stranded, like a fish in a dry pond.
Without—he has not a single farthing of salary:
Within—there is not a peck of grain in his larder.
His relations upbraid him for his lack of success:
His friends and callers daily decrease in number.
Su Ch'in used to go preaching in the North
And Li Ssŭ sent a memorandum to the West.
I once hoped to pluck the fruits of life:
But now alas, they are all withered and dry.
Though one drinks at a river, one cannot drink more
    than a bellyful;
Enough is good, but there is no use in satiety.
The bird in a forest can perch but on one bough,
And this should be the wise man's pattern.

The Desecration of the Han Tombs

By Chang Tsai (third century A.D.)

At Pei-mang how they rise to Heaven,
Those high mounds, four or five in the fields!
What men lie buried under these tombs?
All of them were Lords of the Han world.
"Kung" and "Wēn"[1] gaze across at each other:
The Yüan mound is all grown over with weeds.
When the dynasty was falling, tumult and disorder arose,
Thieves and robbers roamed like wild beasts.
Of earth[2] they have carried away more than one handful,
They have gone into vaults and opened the secret doors.
Jewellèd scabbards lie twisted and defaced:
The stones that were set in them, thieves have carried away,
The ancestral temples are hummocks in the ground:
The walls that went round them are all levelled flat.
Over everything the tangled thorns are growing:
A herd-boy pushes through them up the path.
Down in the thorns rabbits have made their burrows:
The weeds and thistles will never be cleared away.

[1] Names of two tombs.
[2] In the early days of the dynasty a man stole a handful of earth from the imperial tombs, and was executed by the police. The emperor was furious at the lightness of the punishment.

Over the tombs the ploughshare will be driven
And peasants will have their fields and orchards there.
They that were once lords of a thousand hosts
Are now become the dust of the hills and ridges.
I think of what Yün-mēn[1] said
And am sorely grieved at the thought of "then" and "now".

[1] Yün-mēn said to Mēng Ch'ang-chün [died 279 B. c.], "Does it not grieve you to think that after a hundred years this terrace will be cast down and this pond cleared away?" Mēng Ch'ang-chün wept.

Bearer's Song

By Miu Hsi (died A. D. 245)

When I was alive, I wandered in the streets of the Capital:
Now that I am dead, I am left to lie in the fields.
In the morning I drove out from the High Hall:
In the evening I lodged beneath the Yellow Springs.[1]
When the white sun had sunk in the Western Chasm
I hung up my chariot and rested my four horses.
Now, even the mighty Maker of All
Could not bring the life back to my limbs.
Shape and substance day by day will vanish:
Hair and teeth will gradually fall away.
Forever from of old men have been so:
And none born can escape this thing.

Cf. the "Han Burial Songs", p. 33.

[1] Hades.

The Valley Wind

By Lu Yün (A. D. 262–303)

Living in retirement beyond the World,
Silently enjoying isolation,
I pull the rope of my door tighter
And stuff my window with roots and ferns.
My spirit is tuned to the Spring-season:
At the fall of the year there is autumn in my heart.
Thus imitating cosmic changes
My cottage becomes a Universe.

Inviting Guests

By Ch'ēng-kung Sui (died A. D. 273)

I sent out invitations
To summon guests.
I collected together
All my friends.
Loud talk
And simple feasting:
Discussion of philosophy,
Investigation of subtleties.
Tongues loosened
And minds at one.
Hearts refreshed
By discharge of emotion!

Twelve Poems

By T'ao Ch'ien (A. D. 372–427)

[1]

Shady, shady the wood in front of the Hall:
At midsummer full of calm shadows.
The south wind follows summer's train:
With its eddying puffs it blows open my coat.
I am free from ties and can live a life of retirement.
When I rise from sleep, I play with books and harp.
The lettuce in the garden still grows moist:
Of last year's grain there is always plenty left.
Self-support should maintain strict limits:
More than enough is not what I want.
I grind millet and make good wine:
When the wine is heated, I pour it out for myself.
My little children are playing at my side,
Learning to talk, they babble unformed sounds.
These things have made me happy again
And I forget my lost cap of office.
Distant, distant I gaze at the white clouds:
With a deep yearning I think of the Sages of Antiquity.

In the quiet of the morning I heard a knock at my door:
I threw on my clothes and opened it myself.
I asked who it was who had come so early to see me:
He said he was a peasant, coming with good intent.
He brought a present of wine and rice-soup,
Believing that I had fallen on evil days.
"You live in rags under a thatched roof
And seem to have no desire for a better lot.
The rest of mankind have all the same ambitions:
You, too, must learn to wallow in their mire."
"Old man, I am impressed by what you say,
But my soul is not fashioned like other men's.
To drive in their rut I might perhaps learn:
To be untrue to myself could only lead to muddle.
Let us drink and enjoy together the wine you have brought:
For my course is set and cannot now be altered."

[3]

Chill and harsh the year draws to its close:
In my cotton dress I seek sunlight on the porch.
In the southern orchard all the leaves are gone:
In the north garden rotting boughs lie heaped.
I empty my cup and drink it down to the dregs:
I look towards the kitchen, but no smoke rises.
Poems and books lie piled beside my chair:
But the light is going and I shall not have time to read them.
My life here is not like the Agony in Ch'ēn,[1]
But often I have to bear bitter reproaches.
Let me then remember, to calm my heart's distress,
That the Sages of old were often in like case.

[4]

I built my hut in a zone of human habitation,
Yet near me there sounds no noise of horse or coach.
    Would you know how that is possible?
A heart that is distant creates a wilderness round it.
I pluck chrysanthemums under the eastern hedge,
Then gaze long at the distant summer hills.
The mountain air is fresh at the dusk of day:
The flying birds two by two return.
In these things there lies a deep meaning;
Yet when we would express it, words suddenly fail us.

[1] Confucius was maltreated in Ch'ēn.

Blaming Sons

[An Apology for His Own Drunkenness]

White hair covers my temples,
I am wrinkled and seared beyond repair,
And though I have got five sons,
They all hate paper and brush.
A-shu is eighteen:
For laziness there is none like him.
A-hsüan does his best,
But really loathes the Fine Arts.
Yung-tuan is thirteen,
But does not know "six" from "seven".[1]
T'ung-tzŭ in his ninth year
Is only concerned with things to eat.
If Heaven treats me like this,
What can I do but fill my cup?

[1] Written in Chinese with two characters very easy to distinguish.

A long time ago
I went on a journey,
Right to the corner
Of the Eastern Ocean.
The road there
Was long and winding,
And stormy waves
Barred my path.
What made me
Go this way?
Hunger drove me
Into the World.
I tried hard
To fill my belly:
And even a little
Seemed a lot.
But this was clearly
A bad bargain,
So I went home
And lived in idleness.

[7]

Substance, Shadow, and Spirit

High and low, wise and simple, all busily hoard up the
    moments of life. How greatly they err!
Therefore I have to the uttermost exposed the bitterness
    both of Substance and Shadow, and have made
    Spirit show how, by following Nature, we may dis-
    solve this bitterness.

Substance speaks to Shadow:

Heaven and Earth exist for ever:
Mountains and rivers never change.
But herbs and trees in perpetual rotation
Are renovated and withered by the dews and frosts:
And Man the wise, Man the divine—
Shall he alone escape this law?
Fortuitously appearing for a moment in the World
He suddenly departs, never to return.
How can he know that the friends he has left
Are missing him and thinking of him?
Only the things that he used remain;
They look upon them and their tears flow.
Me no magical arts can save,
Though you may hope for a wizard's aid.
I beg you listen to this advice—
When you can get wine, be sure to drink it.

86

Shadow replies:

There is no way to preserve life.
Drugs of Immortality are instruments of folly.
I would gladly wander in Paradise,
But it is far away and there is no road.
Since the day that I was joined to you
We have shared all our joys and pains.
While you rested in the shade, I left you a while:
But till the end we shall be together.
Our joint existence is impermanent:
Sadly together we shall slip away.
That when the body decays Fame should also go
Is a thought unendurable, burning the heart.
Let us strive and labour while yet we may
To do some deed that men will praise.
Wine may in truth dispel our sorrow,
But how compare it with lasting Fame?

Spirit expounds:

God can only set in motion:
He cannot control the things he has made.
Man, the second of the Three Orders,
Owes his precedence to Me.
Though I am different from you,
We were born involved in one another:
Nor by any means can we escape
The intimate sharing of good and ill.

The Three Emperors were saintly men,
Yet to-day—where are they?
P'ēng[1] lived to a great age,
Yet he went at last, when he longed to stay.
And late or soon, all go:
Wise and simple have no reprieve.
Wine may bring forgetfulness,
But does it not hasten old-age?
If you set your hearts on noble deeds,
How do you know that any will praise you?
By all this thinking you do Me injury:
You had better go where Fate leads—
Drift on the Stream of Infinite Flux,
Without joy, without fear:
When you must go—then go,
And make as little fuss as you can.

[8]

Moving House

My old desire to live in the Southern Village
Was not because I had taken a fancy to the house.
But I heard it was a place of simple-minded men
With whom it were a joy to spend the mornings
    and evenings.
Many years I had longed to settle here:

[1] The Chinese Methuselah.

88

Now at last I have managed to move house.
I do not mind if my cottage is rather small
So long as there's room enough for bed and mat.
Often and often the neighbours come to see me
And with brave words discuss the things of old.
Rare writings we read together and praise:
Doubtful meanings we examine together and settle.

[9]

New Corn

Swiftly the years, beyond recall.
Solemn the stillness of this fair morning.
I will clothe myself in spring-clothing
And visit the slopes of the Eastern Hill.
By the mountain-stream a mist hovers,
Hovers a moment, then scatters.
There comes a wind blowing from the south
That brushes the fields of new corn.

[10]

Returning to the Fields

When I was young, I was out of tune with the herd:
My only love was for the hills and mountains.
Unwitting I fell into the Web of the World's dust

And was not free until my thirtieth year.
The migrant bird longs for the old wood:
The fish in the tank thinks of its native pool.
I had rescued from wildness a patch of the Southern Moor
And, still rustic, I returned to field and garden.
My ground covers no more than ten acres:
My thatched cottage has eight or nine rooms.
Elms and willows cluster by the eaves:
Peach trees and plum trees grow before the hall.
Hazy, hazy the distant hamlets of men.
Steady the smoke of the half-deserted village,
A dog barks somewhere in the deep lanes,
A cock crows at the top of the mulberry tree.
At gate and courtyard—no murmur of the World's dust:
In the empty rooms—leisure and deep stillness.
Long I lived checked by the bars of a cage:
Now I have turned again to Nature and Freedom.

[11]

Reading the Book of Hills and Seas

In the month of June the grass grows high
And round my cottage thick-leaved branches sway.
There is not a bird but delights in the place where it rests:
And I too—love my thatched cottage.

I have done my ploughing:
I have sown my seed.
Again I have time to sit and read my books.
In the narrow lane there are no deep ruts:
Often my friends' carriages turn back.
In high spirits I pour out my spring wine
And pluck the lettuce growing in my garden.
A gentle rain comes stealing up from the east
And a sweet wind bears it company.
My thoughts float idly over the story of King Chou.
My eyes wander over the pictures of Hills and Seas.
At a single glance I survey the whole Universe.
He will never be happy, whom such pleasures fail to please!

[12]

Flood

The lingering clouds, rolling, rolling,
And the settled rain, dripping, dripping,
In the Eight Directions—the same dusk.
The level lands—one great river.
Wine I have, wine I have:
Idly I drink at the eastern window.
Longingly—I think of my friends,
But neither boat nor carriage comes.

Climbing A Mountain

By Tao-yün (circa A. D. 400), wife of General Wang Ning-chih.
The general was so stupid that she finally deserted him.

High rises the Eastern Peak
Soaring up to the blue sky.
Among the rocks—an empty hollow,
Secret, still, mysterious!
Uncarved and unhewn,
Screened by nature with a roof of clouds.
    Times and Seasons, what things are you
    Bringing to my life ceaseless change?
    I will lodge for ever in this hollow
    Where Springs and Autumns
        unheeded pass.

Sailing Homeward

By Chan Fang-shēng (fourth century A.D.)

Cliffs that rise a thousand feet
Without a break,
Lake that stretches a hundred miles
Without a wave,
Sands that are white through all the year,
Without a stain,
Pine-tree woods, winter and summer
Ever-green,
Streams that for ever flow and flow
Without a pause,
Trees that for twenty thousand years
Your vows have kept,
You have suddenly healed the pain of a traveller's heart,
And moved his brush to write a new song.

Plucking the Rushes

[*A boy and girl are sent to gather rushes for thatching*]

Anonymous (fourth century A.D.)

Green rushes with red shoots,
Long leaves bending to the wind—
You and I in the same boat
Plucking rushes at the Five Lakes.
We started at dawn from the orchid-island:
We rested under the elms till noon.
You and I plucking rushes
Had not plucked a handful when night came!

Ballad of the Western Island
in the North Country

"Seeing the plum-tree I thought of the Western Island
And I plucked a branch to send to the North Country.
I put on my dress of apricot-yellow silk
And bound up my hair black as the crow's wing.
But which is the road that leads to the Western Island?
I'll ask the man at the ferry by the Bridge of Boats.
But the sun is sinking and the orioles flying home:
And the wind is blowing and sighing in the walnut-tree.
I'll stand under the tree just beside the gate:
I'll stand by the door and show off my enameled hair-pins."
She's opened the gate, but her lover has not come:
She's gone out at the gate to pluck red lotus.
As she plucks the lotus on the southern dyke in autumn,
The lotus flower stands higher than a man's head.
She bends down and plays with the lotus seeds,
The lotus seeds are green like the lake-water.
She gathers the flowers and puts them into her gown—
The lotus-bud that is red all through.
She thinks of her lover, her lover that does not come:
She looks up and sees the wild geese flying—
The Western Island is full of wild geese.
To look for her lover she climbs the Blue Tower.
The tower is high: she looks, but cannot see:

All day she leans on the balcony rails.
The rail is twisted into a twelve-fold pattern.
She lets fall her hand white like the colour of jade.
She rolls up the awning, she sees the wide sky,
And the sea-water waving its vacant blue.
"The sea shall carry my dreams far away,
So that you shall be sorry at last for my sorrow.
If the South wind only knew my thoughts
It would blow my dreams till they got to the Western Island."

The Scholar Recruit

By Pao Chao (died A. D. 466)

Now late
I follow Time's Necessity:[1]
Mounting a barricade I pacify remote tribes.
Discarding my sash I don a coat of hide.
Rolling up my skirts I shoulder a black bow.
Even at the very start my strength fails:
What will become of me before it's all over?

[1] I.e., "enlist".

The Red Hills

By Pao Chao

Red hills lie athwart us as a menace in the west,
And fiery mountains glare terrible in the south.
The body burns, the head aches and throbs:
If a bird light here, its soul forthwith departs.
Warm springs pour from cloudy pools
And hot smoke issues between the rocks.
The sun and moon are perpetually obscured:
The rain and dew never stay dry.
There are red serpents a hundred feet long,
And black snakes ten girths round.
The sand-spitters shoot their poison at the sunbeams:
The flying insects are ill with the shifting glare.
The hungry monkeys dare not come down to eat:
The morning birds dare not set out to fly.
At the Ching river many die of poison:
Crossing the Lu one is lucky if one is only ill.
Our living feet walk on dead ground:
Our high wills surmount the snares of Fate.
The Spear-boat General[1] got but little honour:
The Wave-subduer[2] met with scant reward.
If our Prince still grudges the things that are easy to give,[3]
Can he hope that his soldiers will give what is hardest to give?[4]

[1] Hou Yen (first cent. B. C.).   [2] Ma Yuan (first cent. A. D.).
[3] Rewards and titles.   [4] Life.

Song of the Men of Chin-ling

[*Marching Back into the Capital*]

By Hsieh T'iao (fifth century A. D.)

Chiang-nan is a glorious and beautiful land,
And Chin-ling an exalted and kingly province!
The green canals of the city stretch on and on
And its high towers stretch up and up.
Flying gables lean over the bridle-road:
Drooping willows cover the Royal Aqueduct.
Shrill flutes sing by the coach's awning,
And reiterated drums bang near its painted wheels.
The names of the deserving shall be carved on the
     Cloud Terrace.[1]
And for those who have done valiantly rich
     reward awaits.

[1] The Record Office.

Song

By Tsang Chih (*sixth century A. D.*)

I was brought up under the Stone Castle:
My window opened on to the castle tower.
In the castle were beautiful young men
Who waved to me as they went in and out.

Dreaming of a Dead Lady

"I heard at night your long sighs
And knew that you were thinking of me."
As she spoke, the doors of Heaven opened
And our souls conversed and I saw her face.
She set me a pillow to rest on
And she brought me meat and drink.

I stood beside her where she lay,
But suddenly woke and she was not there:
And none knew how my soul was torn,
How the tears fell surging over my breast.

The Liberator

[A Political Allegory]

By Wu-ti, Emperor of the Liang dynasty (A. D. 464–549)

In the high trees—many doleful winds:
The ocean waters—lashed into waves.
If the sharp sword be not in your hand,
How can you hope your friends will remain many?
Do you not see that sparrow on the fence?
Seeing the hawk it casts itself into the snare.
The fowler to catch the sparrow is delighted:
The Young Man to see the sparrow is grieved.
He takes his sword and cuts through the netting:
The yellow sparrow flies away, away.
Away, away, up to the blue sky
And down again to thank the Young Man.

Lo-yang

By the Emperor Ch'ien Wên-ti (sixth century A. D.)

A beautiful place is the town of Lo-yang:
The big streets are full of spring light.
The lads go driving out with harps in their hands:
The mulberry girls go out to the fields with their baskets.
Golden whips glint at the horses' flanks,
Gauze sleeves brush the green boughs.
Racing dawn, the carriages come home,—
And the girls with their high baskets full of fruit.

People Hide Their Love

By Wu-ti

Who says
That it's by my desire,
This separation, this living so far from you?
My dress still smells of the lavender you gave:
My hand still holds the letter that you sent.
Round my waist I wear a double sash:
I dream that it binds us both with a same-heart knot.
Did not you know that people hide their love,
Like the flower that seems too precious to be picked?

The Rejected Wife

By Yüan-ti (A. D. 508–554)

Entering the Hall, she meets the new wife:
Leaving the gate, she runs into her former husband.
Words stick: she does not manage to say anything:
She presses her hands together and hesitates.
Agitates moon-like fan—sheds pearl-like tears—
Realizes she loves him just as much as ever:
That her present pain will never come to an end.

The Ferry

By the Emperor Ch'ien Wên-ti, of the Liang dynasty,
who reigned during the year A. D. 500.

Of marsh-mallows my boat is made,
The ropes are lily-roots.
The pole-star is athwart the sky:
The moon sinks low.
It's at the ferry I'm plucking lilies,
But it might be the Yellow River—
So afraid you seem of the wind and waves,
So long you tarry at the crossing.[1]

[1] A lady is waiting for her lover at the ferry which crosses a small stream.
When he does not come, she bitterly suggests that he is as afraid of the
little stream as though it were the Yellow River, the largest river in
China.

The Waters of Lung-t'ou

[The North-west Frontier]

By Hsü Ling (A. D. 507–583)

The road that I came by mounts eight thousand feet:
The river that I crossed hangs a hundred fathoms.
The brambles so thick that in summer one cannot pass!
The snow so high that in winter one cannot climb!
With branches that interlace Lung Valley is dark:
Against cliffs that tower one's voice beats and echoes.
I turn my head, and it seems only a dream
That I ever lived in the streets of Hsien-yang.

Flowers and Moonlight
on the Spring River

By Yang-ti (A. D. 605–617), Emperor of the Sui dynasty

The evening river is level and motionless—
The spring colours just open to their full.
Suddenly a wave carries the moon[1] away
And the tidal water comes with its freight of stars.[1]

[1] *I.e.*, the reflection in the water.

108

Winter Night

My bed is so empty that I keep on waking up:
As the cold increases, the night-wind begins to blow.
It rustles the curtains, making a noise like the sea:
Oh that those were waves which could carry me back to you!

Tchirek Song

Altun (A. D. 486-566) was a Tartar employed by the
Chinese in drilling their troops "after the manner of the Huns".
He could not read or write. The "Yo Fu Kuang T'i" says: Kao
Huan attacked Pi, king of Chou, but lost nearly half his men. Kao
Huan fell ill of sadness and Pi, to taunt him, sent out a proclamation,
which said:

> Kao Huan, that son of a mouse
> Dared to attack King Pi.
> But at the first stroke of sword and bow,
> The aggressor's plot recoiled on himself.

When this reached Kao Huan's ears, he sat up in bed and tried to comfort his officers. All the nobles were summoned to his room, and Altun was asked to sing them a song about Tchirek, his native land.

He sang:

Tchirek River
Lies under the Dark Mountains:
Where the sky is like the sides of a tent
Stretched down over the Great Steppe.
The sky is gray, gray:
And the steppe wide, wide:
Over grass that the wind has battered low
Sheep and oxen roam.

"Altun" means "gold" in Tartar. No one could teach him to write the Chinese character for gold, till at last some one said: "Draw the roof of your house and then put a few strokes underneath." He thus learnt, in a rough fashion, to write his own name.

Business Men

By Ch'ēn Tzŭ-ang (A.D. 656-698)

Business men boast of their skill and cunning
But in philosophy they are like little children.
Bragging to each other of successful depredations
They neglect to consider the ultimate fate of the body.
What should they know of the Master of Dark Truth
Who saw the wide world in a jade cup,
By illumined conception got clear of Heaven and Earth:
On the chariot of Mutation entered the Gate of Immutability?

112

On Going to a Tavern

By Wang Chi

These days, continually fuddled with drink,
I fail to satisfy the appetites of the soul.
But seeing men all behaving like drunkards,[1]
How can I alone remain sober?

[1] Written during the war which preceded the T'ang dynasty.

Tell Me Now

By Wang Chi (A. D. 584-644)

"Tell me now, what should a man want
But to sit alone, sipping his cup of wine?"
I should like to have visitors come and discuss philosophy
And not to have the tax-collector coming to collect taxes:
My three sons married into good families
And my five daughters wedded to steady husbands.
Then I could jog through a happy five-score years
And, at the end, need no Paradise.

Stone Fish Lake

By Yüan Chieh (flourished circa A. D. 723-772)

Yüan Chieh, a contemporary of Li Po, has not hitherto been mentioned in any European book. "His subjects were always original, but his poems are seldom worth quoting," is a Chinese opinion of him.

I loved you dearly, Stone Fish Lake,
With your rock-island shaped like a swimming fish!
On the fish's back is the Wine-cup Hollow
And round the fish,—the flowing waters of the Lake.
The boys on the shore sent little wooden ships,
Each made to carry a single cup of wine.
The island-drinkers emptied the liquor-boats
And set their sails and sent them back for more.
On the shores of the Lake were jutting slabs of rock
And under the rocks there flowed an icy stream.
Heated with wine to rinse our mouths and hands
In those cold waters was a joy beyond compare!

Of gold and jewels I have not any need;
For Caps and Coaches I do not care at all.
But I wish I could sit on the rocky banks of the Lake
For ever and ever staring at the Stone Fish.

Prose Letter

By Wang Wei (A. D. 699–759)

To the Bachelor-of-Arts P'ei Ti

OF LATE during the sacrificial month, the weather has been calm and clear, and I might easily have crossed the mountain. But I knew that you were conning the classics and did not dare disturb you. So I roamed about the mountain-side, rested at the Kan-p'ei Temple, dined with the mountain priests, and, after dinner, came home again. Going northwards, I crossed the Yüan-pa, over whose waters the unclouded moon shone with dazzling rim. When night was far advanced, I mounted Hua-tzŭ's Hill and saw the moonlight tossed up and thrown down by the jostling waves of Wang River. On the wintry mountain distant lights twinkled and vanished; in some deep lane beyond the forest a dog barked at the cold, with a cry as fierce as a wolf's. The sound of villagers grinding their corn at night filled the gaps between the slow chiming of a distant bell.

Now I am sitting alone. I listen, but cannot hear my grooms and servants move or speak. I think much of old days: how hand in hand, composing poems as we went, we walked down twisting paths to the banks of clear streams.

We must wait for Spring to come: till the grasses sprout and the trees bloom. Then wandering together in the spring

116

hills we shall see the trout leap lightly from the stream, the white gulls stretch their wings, the dew fall on the green moss. And in the morning we shall hear the cry of curlews in the barley-fields.

It is not long to wait. Shall you be with me then? Did I not know the natural subtlety of your intelligence, I would not dare address to you so remote an invitation. You will understand that a deep feeling dictates this course.

Written without disrespect by Wang Wei, a dweller in the mountains.

Drinking Alone by Moonlight

Three Poems by Li Po (A. D. 701-762)

[1]

A cup of wine, under the flowering trees;
I drink alone, for no friend is near.
Raising my cup I beckon the bright moon,
For he, with my shadow, will make three men.
The moon, alas, is no drinker of wine;
Listless, my shadow creeps about at my side.
Yet with the moon as friend and the shadow as slave
I must make merry before the Spring is spent.
To the songs I sing the moon flickers her beams;
In the dance I weave my shadow tangles and breaks.
While we were sober, three shared the fun;
Now we are drunk, each goes his way.
May we long share our odd, inanimate feast,
And meet at last on the Cloudy River of the sky.[1]

[1] The Milky Way.

118

[2]

In the third month the town of Hsien-yang
Is thick-spread with a carpet of fallen flowers.
Who in Spring can bear to grieve alone?
Who, sober, look on sights like these?
Riches and Poverty, long or short life,
By the Maker of Things are portioned and disposed;
But a cup of wine levels life and death
And a thousand things obstinately hard to prove.
When I am drunk, I lose Heaven and Earth.
Motionless—I cleave to my lonely bed.
At last I forget that I exist at all,
And at *that* moment my joy is great indeed.

[3]

If High Heaven had no love for wine,
There would not be a Wine Star in the sky.
If Earth herself had no love for wine,
There would not be a city called Wine Springs.[1]
Since Heaven and Earth both love wine,
I can love wine, without shame before God.
Clear wine was once called "a Saint";[2]
Thick wine was once called "a Sage".[2]

Of Saint and Sage I have long quaffed deep,
What need for me to study spirits and *hsien*?[3]
At the third cup I penetrate the Great Way;
A full gallon—Nature and I are one . . .
But the things I feel when wine possesses my soul
I will never tell to those who are not drunk.

[1] Ch'iu-ch'üan, in Kansuh.
[2] "History of Wei Dynasty" (Life of Hsü Mo): "A drunken visitor said,
'Clear wine I account a Saint: thick wine only a Sage'."
[3] The lore of Rishi, Immortals.

120

In the Mountains on
A Summer Day

By Li Po

Gently I stir a white feather fan,
With open shirt sitting in a green wood.
I take off my cap and hang it on a jutting stone;
A wind from the pine-trees trickles on my bare head.

Self-Abandonment

By Li Po

I sat drinking and did not notice the dusk,
Till falling petals filled the folds of my dress.
Drunken I rose and walked to the moonlit stream;
The birds were gone, and men also few.

Waking from Drunkenness on a Spring Day

By Li Po

"Life in the World is but a big dream;
I will not spoil it by any labour or care."
So saying, I was drunk all the day,
Lying helpless at the porch in front of my door.
When I woke up, I blinked at the garden-lawn;
A lonely bird was singing amid the flowers.
I asked myself, had the day been wet or fine?
The Spring wind was telling the mango-bird.
Moved by its song I soon began to sigh,
And as wine was there I filled my own cup.
Wildly singing I waited for the moon to rise;
When my song was over, all my senses had gone.

To Tan Ch'iu

By Li Po

My friend is lodging high in the Eastern Range,
Dearly loving the beauty of valleys and hills.
At green Spring he lies in the empty woods,
And is still asleep when the sun shines on high.
A pine-tree wind dusts his sleeves and coat;
A pebbly stream cleans his heart and ears.
I envy you, who far from strife and talk
Are high-propped on a pillow of blue cloud.

Clearing at Dawn

By Li Po

The fields are chill; the sparse rain has stopped;
The colours of Spring teem on every side.
With leaping fish the blue pond is full;
With singing thrushes the green boughs droop.
The flowers of the field have dabbled their
    powdered cheeks;
The mountain grasses are bent level at the waist.
By the bamboo stream the last fragment of cloud
Blown by the wind slowly scatters away.

Poems by Po Chü-i

Life of Po Chü-i

772 Born on 20th of 1st month.

800 Passes his examinations.

806 Receives a minor post at Chou-chih, near the capital.

807 Made Scholar of the Han Lin Academy.

811 Retires to Wei River, being in mourning for his mother.

814 Returns to Court.

815 Banished to Hsün-yang.

818 Removed to Chung-chou.

820 Reprieved and returns to Court.

822 Governor of Hangchow.

825 Governor of Soochow.

826 Retires owing to illness.

827 Returns to Ch'ang-an.

829 Settles permanently at Lo-yang.

831 Governor of Honan, the province of which Lo-yang was capital.

833 Retires owing to illness.

839 Has paralytic stroke in tenth month.

846 Dies in the eighth month.

Introduction

PO CHÜ-I was born at T'ai-yüan in Shansi. Most of his childhood was spent at Jung-yang in Honan. His father was a second-class Assistant Department Magistrate. He tells us that his family was poor and often in difficulties.

He seems to have settled permanently at Ch'ang-an in 801. This town, lying near the north-west frontier, was the political capital of the Empire. In its situation it somewhat resembled Madrid. Lo-yang, the Eastern city, owing to its milder climate and more accessible position, became, like Seville in Spain, a kind of *social* capital.

Soon afterwards he met Yüan Chēn, then aged twenty-two, who was destined to play so important a part in his life. Five years later, during a temporary absence from the city, he addressed to Yüan the following poem:

> Since I left my home to seek official state
> Seven years I have lived in Ch'ang-an.
> What have I gained? Only you, Yüan;
> So hard it is to bind friendships fast.
> We have roamed on horseback under the flowering trees;
> We have walked in the snow and warmed our hearts with wine.
> We have met and parted at the Western Gate
> And neither of us bothered to put on Cap or Belt.
> We did not go up together for Examination;
> We were not serving in the same Department of State.

127

The bond that joined us lay deeper than outward things;
The rivers of our souls spring from the same well!

Of Yüan's appearance at this time we may guess something from a picture which still survives in copy; it shows
him, a youthful and elegant figure, visiting his cousin Ts'ui
Ying-ying, who was a lady-in-waiting at Court.[1] At this
period of his life Po made friends with difficulty, not being,
as he tells us "a master of such accomplishments as calligraphy,
painting, chess or gambling, which tend to bring men together
in pleasurable intercourse". Two older men, T'ang Ch'ü and
Tēng Fang, liked his poetry and showed him much kindness;
another, the politician K'ung T'an, won his admiration on
public grounds. But all three died soon after he got to know
them. Later he made three friends with whom he maintained
a lifelong intimacy: the poet Liu Yü-hsi (called Mēng-tē), and
the two officials Li Chien and Ts'ui Hsuan-liang. In 805 Yüan
Chēn was banished for provocative behaviour towards a high
official. The T'ang History relates the episode as follows:
"Yüan was staying the night at the Fu-shui Inn; just as he was
preparing to go to sleep in the Main Hall, the court-official Li
Shih-yüan also arrived. Yüan Chēn should have offered to
withdraw from the Hall. He did not do so and a scuffle en-
sued. Yüan, locked out of the building, took off his shoes and
stole round to the back, hoping to find another way in. Li followed with a whip and struck him across the face."

[1] Yüan told of this intrigue in the 'Story of Ts'ui Ying-ying'. See p. 299. Upon
this fragment is founded the famous XIV cent. drama, 'The Western Pavilion'.

128

The separation was a heavy blow to Po Chü-i. In a poem called "Climbing Alone to the Lo-yu Gardens" he says:

> I look down on the Twelve City Streets: —
> Red dust flanked by green trees!
> Coaches and horsemen alone fill my eyes;
> I do not see whom my heart longs to see.
> K'ung T'an has died at Lo-yang;
> Yüan Chēn is banished to Ching-mēn. . . .

In 804 on the death of his father, and again in 811 on the death of his mother, he spent periods of retirement on the Wei River near Ch'ang-an. It was during the second of these periods that he wrote the long poem (260 lines) called "Visiting the Wuchēn Temple". Soon after his return to Ch'ang-an, which took place in the winter of 814, he fell into official disfavour. In two long memorials entitled "On Stopping the War", he had criticized the handling of a campaign against an unimportant tribe of Tartars, which he considered had been unduly prolonged. In a series of poems he had satirized the rapacity of minor officials and called attention to the intolerable sufferings of the masses.

His enemies soon found an opportunity of silencing him. In 814 the Prime Minister, Wu Yüan-hēng, was assassinated in broad daylight by an agent of the revolutionary leader Wu Yüan-chi. Po, in a memorial to the Throne, pointed out the urgency of remedying the prevailing discontent. He held at this time the post of assistant secretary to the Princes' tutor. He should not have criticized the Prime Minister (for being murdered!) until the official Censors had spoken, for he held a Palace appointment which did not carry with it the right of censorship.

His opponents also raked up another charge. His mother had met her death by falling into a well while looking at flowers. Chü-i had written two poems entitled "In Praise of Flowers" and "The New Well". It was claimed that by choosing such subjects he had infringed the laws of Filial Piety. He was banished to Kiukiang (then called Hsün-yang) with the rank of Sub-Prefect. After three years he was given the Governorship of Chung-chou, a remote place in Ssech'uan. On the way up the Yangtze he met Yüan Chēn after three years of separation. They spent a few days together at I-ch'ang, exploring the rock-caves of the neighbourhood.

Chung-chou is noted for its "many flowers and exotic trees", which were a constant delight to its new Governor. In the winter of 819 he was recalled to the capital and became a second-class Assistant Secretary. About this time Yüan Chēn also returned to the city.

In 821 the Emperor Mou Tsung came to the throne. His arbitrary mis-government soon caused a fresh rising in the north-west. Chü-i remonstrated in a series of memorials and was again removed from the capital—this time to be Governor of the important town of Hangchow. Yüan now held a judicial post at Ningpo and the two were occasionally able to meet.

In 824 his Governorship expired and he lived (with the nominal rank of Imperial Tutor) at the village of Li-tao-li, near Lo-yang. It was here that he took into his household two girls, Fan-su and Man-tzŭ, whose singing and dancing enlivened his retreat. He also brought with him from Hangchow a famous "Indian rock", and two cranes of the celebrated "Hua-t'ing" breed. Other amenities of his life at this time were a recipe for making sweet wine, the gift of Ch'ēn Hao-hsien; a harp-melody taught him by Ts'ui Hsuan-liang; and a song called "Autumn Thoughts", brought by the concubine of a visitor from Ssech'uan.

131

In 825 he became Governor of Soochow. Here at the age of fifty-three he enjoyed a kind of second youth, much more sociable than that of thirty years before; we find him end-lessly picnicking and feasting. But after two years illness obliged him to retire.

He next held various posts at the capital, but again fell ill, and in 829 settled at Lo-yang as Governor of the Province of Honan. Here his first son, A-ts'ui, was born, but died in the following year.

In 831 Yüan Chēn also died.

Henceforth, though for thirteen years he continued to hold nominal posts, he lived a life of retirement. In 832 he repaired an unoccupied part of the Hsiang-shan monastery at Lung-mēn,[1] a few miles south of Lo-yang, and lived there, calling himself the Hermit of Hsiang-shan. Once he invited to dinner eight other elderly and retired officials; the occasion was recorded in a picture entitled "The Nine Old Men at Hsiang-shan". There is no evidence that his association with them was otherwise than transient, though legend (see "Mémoires Concernant les Chinois" and Giles, "Biographical Dictionary") has invested the incident with an undue impor-tance. He amused himself at this time by writing a description of his daily life which would be more interesting if it were not so closely modelled on a famous memoir by T'ao Ch'ien. In the winter of 839 he was attacked by paralysis and lost the use of his left leg. After many months in bed he was again able to visit his garden, carried by Ju-man, a favourite monk.

[1] Famous for its rock-sculptures, carved in the sixth and seventh centuries.

In 842 Liu Yü-hsi, the last survivor of the four friends, and a constant visitor at the monastery, "went to wander with Yüan Chēn in Hades". The monk Ju-man also died.

The remaining years of Po's life were spent in collecting and arranging his Complete Works. Copies were presented to the principal monasteries (the "Public Libraries" of the period) in the towns with which he had been connected. He died in 846, leaving instructions that his funeral should be without pomp and that he should be buried not in the family tomb at Hsia-kuei, but by Ju-man's side in the Hsiang-shan Monastery. He desired that a posthumous title should not be awarded.

The most striking characteristic of Po Chü-i's poetry is its verbal simplicity. There is a story that he was in the habit of reading his poems to an old peasant woman and altering any expression which she could not understand. The poems of his contemporaries were mere elegant diversions which enabled the scholar to display his erudition, or the literary juggler his dexterity. Po expounded his theory of poetry in a letter to Yüan Chēn. Like Confucius, he regarded art solely as a method of conveying instruction. He is not the only great artist who has advanced this untenable theory. He accordingly valued his didactic poems far above his other work; but it is obvious that much of his best poetry conveys no moral whatever. He admits, indeed, that among his "miscellaneous stanzas" many were inspired by some momentary sensation or passing event. "A single laugh or a single sigh were rapidly translated into verse".

133

The didactic poems or "satires" belong to the period before his first banishment. "When the tyrants and favourites heard my Songs of Ch'in, they looked at one another and changed countenance", he boasts. Satire, in the European sense, implies *wit*; but Po's satires are as lacking in true wit as they are unquestionably full of true poetry. We must regard them simply as moral tales in verse.

In the conventional lyric poetry of his predecessors he finds little to admire. Among the earlier poems of the T'ang dynasty he selects for praise the series by Ch'ēn Tzǔ-ang, which includes "Business Men". In Li Po and Tu Fu he finds a deficiency of "fēng" and "ya". The two terms are borrowed from the Preface to the Odes. "Fēng" means "criticism of one's rules"; "ya", "moral guidance to the masses".

"The skill", he says in the same letter, "which Tu Fu shows in threading on to his *Lü-shih* ramification of allusions ancient and modern could not be surpassed; in this he is even superior to Li Po. But, if we take the 'Press-gang' and verses like that stanza:

At the palace doors the smell of meat and wine;
On the road the bones of one who was frozen to death.

what a small part of his whole work it represents!"

Content, in short, he valued far above form: and it was part of his theory, though certainly not of his practice, that this content ought to be definitely moral. He aimed at raising poetry from the triviality into which it had sunk and restoring it to its proper intellectual level. It is an irony that he should be chiefly known to posterity, in China, Japan, and the West,

134

as the author of the "Everlasting Wrong".[1] He set little store by the poem himself, and, though a certain political moral might be read into it, its appeal is clearly romantic.

His other poem of sentiment, the "Lute Girl",[2] accords even less with his stated principles. With these he ranks his *Lü-shih*; and it should here be noted that all the satires and long poems are in the old style of versification, while his lighter poems are in the strict, modern form. With his satires he classes his "reflective" poems, such as "Singing in the Mountains", "On Being Removed from Hsün-yang", "Pruning Trees", etc. These are all in the old style.

No poet in the world can ever have enjoyed greater contemporary popularity than Po. His poems were "on the mouths of kings, princes, concubines, ladies, plough-boys, and grooms". They were inscribed "on the walls of village-schools, temples, and ships-cabins". "A certain Captain Kao Hsia-yü was courting a dancing-girl. 'You must not think I am an ordinary dancing-girl', she said to him, 'I can recite Master Po's "Everlasting Wrong"'. And she put up her price".

But this popularity was confined to the long, romantic poems and the *Lü-shih*. "The world", writes Po to Yüan Chēn, "values highest just those of my poems which I most despise. Of contemporaries you alone have understood my satires and reflective poems. A hundred, a thousand years hence perhaps some one will come who will understand them as you have done".

[1] Giles, "Chinese Literature", p. 169. [2] *Ibid.*, p. 165.

The popularity of his lighter poems lasted till the Ming dynasty, when a wave of pedantry swept over China. At that period his poetry was considered vulgar, because it was not erudite; and prosaic, because it was not rhetorical. Although they valued form far above content, not even the Ming critics can accuse him of slovenly writing. His versification is admitted by them to be "correct".

Caring, indeed, more for matter than for manner, he used with facility and precision the technical instruments which were at his disposal. Many of the later anthologies omit his name altogether, but he has always had isolated admirers. Yüan Mei imitates him constantly, and Chao I (died 1814) writes: "Those who accuse him of being vulgar and prosaic know nothing of poetry."

Even during his lifetime his reputation had reached Japan, and great writers like Michizane were not ashamed to borrow from him. He is still held in high repute there, is the subject of a Nō Play and has even become a kind of Shintō deity. It is significant that the only copy of his works in the British Museum is a seventeenth-century Japanese edition.

It is usual to close a biographical notice with an attempt to describe the "character" of one's subject. But I hold myself absolved from such a task; for the poems which follow will enable the reader to perform it for himself.

Resignation

Keep off your thoughts from things that are past and done;
For thinking of the past wakes regret and pain.
Keep off your thoughts from thinking what will happen;
To think of the future fills one with dismay.
Better by day to sit like a sack in your chair;
Better by night to lie a stone in your bed.
When food comes, then open your mouth;
When sleep comes, then close your eyes.

After Passing the Examination

(A. D. 800)

For ten years I never left my books;
I went up . . . and won unmerited praise.
My high place I do not much prize;
The joy of my parents will first make me proud.
Fellow students, six or seven men,
See me off as I leave the City gate.
My covered couch is ready to drive away;
Flutes and strings blend their parting tune.
Hopes achieved dull the pains of parting;
Fumes of wine shorten the long road . . .
Shod with wings is the horse of him who rides
On a Spring day the road that leads to home.

Escorting Candidates to the Examination Hall

(A. D. 805)

At dawn I rode to escort the Doctors of Art;
In the eastern quarter the sky was still grey.
I said to myself, "You have started far too soon,"
But horses and coaches already thronged the road.
High and low the riders' torches bobbed;
Muffled or loud, the watchman's drum beat.
      Riders, when I see you prick
To your early levee, pity fills my heart.
When the sun rises and the hot dust flies
And the creatures of earth resume their great strife,
You, with your striving, what shall you each seek?
Profit and fame, for that is all your care.
But I, you courtiers, rise from my bed at noon
And live idly in the city of Ch'ang-an.
Spring is deep and my term of office spent;
Day by day my thoughts go back to the hills.

In Early Summer Lodging in
A Temple to Enjoy the Moonlight

(A. D. 805)

In early summer, with two or three more
That were seeking fame in the city of Ch'ang-an,
Whose low employ gave them less business
Than ever they had since first they left their homes,—
With these I wandered deep into the shrine of Tao,
For the joy we sought was promised in this place.
When we reached the gate, we sent our coaches back;
We entered the yard with only cap and stick.
Still and clear, the first weeks of May,
When trees are green and bushes soft and wet;
When the wind has stolen the shadows of new leaves
And birds linger on the last boughs that bloom.
Towards evening when the sky grew clearer yet
And the South-east was still clothed in red,
To the western cloister we carried our jar of wine;
While we waited for the moon, our cups moved slow.
Soon, how soon her golden ghost was born,
Swiftly, as though she had waited for us to come.

140

The beams of her light shone in every place,
On towers and halls dancing to and fro.
Till day broke we sat in her clear light
Laughing and singing, and yet never grew tired.
In Ch'ang-an, the place of profit and fame,
Such moods as this, how many men know?

Sick Leave

(While Secretary to the Deputy-Assistant-Magistrate
of Chou-chih, near Ch'ang-an, in A.D. 806)

Propped on pillows, not attending to business;
For two days I've lain behind locked doors.
I begin to think that those who hold office
Get no rest, except by falling ill!
For restful thoughts one does not need space;
The room where I lie is ten foot square.
By the western eaves, above the bamboo-twigs,
From my couch I see the White Mountain rise.
But the clouds that hover on its far-distant peak
Bring shame to a face that is buried in the World's dust.

Watching the Reapers

(A. D. 806)

Tillers of the soil have few idle months;
In the fifth month their toil is double-fold.
A south-wind visits the fields at night:
Suddenly the hill is covered with yellow corn.
Wives and daughters shoulder baskets of rice;
Youths and boys carry the flasks of wine.
Following after they bring a wage of meat
To the strong reapers toiling on the southern hill,
Whose feet are burned by the hot earth they tread,
Whose backs are scorched by flames of the shining sky.
Tired they toil, caring nothing for the heat,
Grudging the shortness of the long summer day.
A poor woman follows at the reapers' side
With an infant child carried close at her breast.
With her right hand she gleans the fallen grain;
On her left arm a broken basket hangs.
And I to-day . . . by virtue of what right
Have I never once tended field or tree?
My government-pay is three hundred tons;
At the year's end I have still grain in hand.
Thinking of this, secretly I grew ashamed;
And all day the thought lingered in my head.

Going Alone to Spend a Night
at the Hsien-yu Temple

(A.D. 806)

The crane from the shore standing at the top of the steps;
The moon on the pool seen at the open door;
Where these are, I made my lodging-place
And for two nights could not turn away.
I am glad I chanced on a place so lonely and still
With no companion to drag me early home.
Now that I have tasted the joy of being alone
I will never again come with a friend at my side.

Planting Bamboos
(A. D. 806)

Unrewarded, my will to serve the State;
At my closed door autumn grasses grow.
What could I do to ease a rustic heart?
I planted bamboos, more than a hundred shoots.
When I see their beauty, as they grow by the stream-side,
I feel again as though I lived in the hills,
And many a time on public holidays
Round their railing I walk till night comes.
Do not say that their roots are still weak,
Do not say that their shade is still small;
Already I feel that both in garden and house
Day by day a fresher air moves.
But most I love, lying near the window-side,
To hear in their branches the sound of the autumn-wind.

To Li Chien

(*Part of a Poem, A.D. 807*)

Worldly matters again draw my steps;
Worldly things again seduce my heart.
Whenever for long I part from Li Chien
Gradually my thoughts grow narrow and covetous.
I remember how once I used to visit you;
I stopped my horse and tapped at the garden-gate.
Often when I came you were still lying in bed;
Your little children were sent to let me in.
And you, laughing, ran to the front-door
With coat-tails flying and cap all awry.
On the swept terrace, green patterns of moss;
On the dusted bench, clean shadows of leaves.
To gaze at the hills we sat in the eastern lodge;
To wait for the moon we walked to the southern moor.
At your quiet gate only birds spoke;
In your distant street few drums were heard.
Opposite each other all day we talked,
And never once spoke of profit or fame.
Since we parted hands, how long has passed?
Thrice and again the full moon has shone.
For when we parted the last flowers were falling,
And to-day I hear new cicadas sing.
The scented year suddenly draws to its close,
Yet the sorrow of parting is still unsubdued.

145

An Early Levée

[*Addressed to Ch'ēn, the Hermit*]

At Ch'ang-an—a full foot of snow;
A levée at dawn—to bestow congratulations on the Emperor.
Just as I was nearing the Gate of the Silver Terrace,
After I had left the suburb of Hsin-ch'ang
On the high causeway my horse's foot slipped;
In the middle of the journey my lantern suddenly went out.
Ten leagues riding, always facing to the North;
The cold wind almost blew off my ears.
I waited for the bell outside the Five Gates;
I waited for the summons within the Triple Hall.
My hair and beard were frozen and covered with icicles;
My coat and robe—chilly like water.
Suddenly I thought of Hsien-yu Valley
And secretly envied Ch'ēn Chü-shih,
In warm bed-socks dozing beneath the rugs
And not getting up till the sun has mounted the sky.

Being on Duty all Night in the Palace and Dreaming of Hsien-yu Temple

At the western window I paused from writing rescripts;
The pines and bamboos were all buried in stillness.
The moon rose and a calm wind came;
Suddenly, it was like an evening in the hills.
And so, as I dozed, I dreamed of the South West
And thought I was staying at the Hsien-yu Temple.[1]
When I woke and heard the dripping of the Palace clock
I still thought it the murmur of a mountain stream.

[1] Where the poet used to spend his holidays.

The Letter

Preface: After I parted with Yüan Chēn, I suddenly dreamt
one night that I saw him. When I awoke, I found that a
letter from him had just arrived and, enclosed in it, a
poem on the *paulovnia* flower.

We talked together in the Yung-shou Temple;
We parted to the north of the Hsin-ch'ang dyke.
Going home—I shed a few tears,
Grieving about things,—not sorry for you.
Long, long the road to Lan-t'ien;
You said yourself you would not be able to write.
Reckoning up your halts for eating and sleeping—
By this time you've crossed the Shang mountains.
Last night the clouds scattered away;
A thousand leagues, the same moonlight scene.
When dawn came, I dreamt I saw your face;
It must have been that you were thinking of me.
In my dream, I thought I held your hand
And asked you to tell me what your thoughts were.
And *you* said: "I miss you bitterly,
But there's no one here to send to you with a letter."
When I awoke, before I had time to speak,
A knocking on the door sounded "Doong, doong!"
They came and told me a messenger from Shang-chou
Had brought a letter,—a single scroll from you!

148

Up from my pillow I suddenly sprang out of bed,
And threw on my clothes, all topsy-turvy.
I undid the knot and saw the letter within;
A single sheet with thirteen lines of writing.
At the top it told the sorrows of an exile's heart;
At the bottom it described the pains of separation.
The sorrows and pains took up so much space
There was no room left to talk about the weather!
    But you said that when you wrote
You were staying for the night to the east of Shang-chou;
Sitting alone, lighted by a solitary candle
Lodging in the mountain hostel of Yang-Ch'ēng.
    Night was late when you finished writing,
The mountain moon was slanting towards the west.
What is it lies aslant across the moon?
A single tree of purple *paulovnia* flowers,
Paulovnia flowers just on the point of falling
Are a symbol to express "thinking of an absent friend".
Lovingly—you wrote on the back side,
To send in the letter, your "Poem of the Paulovnia Flower".
The "Poem of the Paulovnia Flower" has eight rhymes;
Yet these eight couplets have cast a spell on my heart.
They have taken hold of this morning's thoughts
And carried them to yours, the night you wrote your letter.
The whole poem I read three times;
Each verse ten times I recite.
So precious to me are the fourscore words
That each letter changes into a bar of gold!

Passing T'ien-mēn Street in Ch'ang-an and Seeing a Distant View of Chung-nan Mountain

The snow has gone from Chung-nan[1]; spring is almost come.
Lovely in the distance its blue colours, against the brown
    of the streets.
A thousand coaches, ten thousand horsemen pass down the
    Nine Roads;
Turns his head and looks at the mountains,—not one man!

[1] Part of the great Nan Shan range, fifteen miles south of Ch'ang-an.

Rejoicing at the Arrival of
Ch'ēn Hsiung

(Circa A. D. 812)

When the yellow bird's note was almost stopped;
And half formed the green plum's fruit;
Sitting and grieving that spring things were over,
I rose and entered the Eastern Garden's gate.
I carried my cup and was dully drinking alone:
Suddenly I heard a knocking sound at the door.
Dwelling secluded, I was glad that someone had come;
How much the more, when I saw it was Ch'ēn Hsiung!
At ease and leisure,—all day we talked;
Crowding and jostling, the feelings of many years.
How great a thing is a single cup of wine!
For it makes us tell the story of our whole lives.

Golden Bells

When I was almost forty
I had a daughter whose name was Golden Bells.
Now it is just a year since she was born;
She is learning to sit and cannot yet talk.
Ashamed,—to find that I have not a sage's heart:
I cannot resist vulgar thoughts and feelings.
Henceforward I am tied to things outside myself:
My only reward,—the pleasure I am getting now.
If I am spared the grief of her dying young,
Then I shall have the trouble of getting her married.
My plan for retiring and going back to the hills
Must now be postponed for fifteen years!

Remembering Golden Bells

Ruined and ill,—a man of two score;
    Pretty and guileless,—a girl of three.
Not a boy,—but still better than nothing:
To soothe one's feeling,—from time to time a kiss!
There came a day,—they suddenly took her from me;
Her soul's shadow wandered I know not where.
And when I remember how just at the time she died
She lisped strange sounds, beginning to learn to talk,
Then I know that the ties of flesh and blood
Only bind us to a load of grief and sorrow.
At last, by thinking of the time before she was born,
By thought and reason I drove the pain away.
Since my heart forgot her, many days have passed
And three times winter has changed to spring.
This morning, for a little, the old grief came back,
Because, in the road, I met her foster-nurse.

Illness

Sad, sad—lean with long illness;
Monotonous, monotonous—days and nights pass.
The summer trees have clad themselves in shade;
The autumn "lan"[1] already houses the dew.
The eggs that lay in the nest when I took to bed
Have changed into little birds and flown away.
The worm that then lay hidden in its hole
Has hatched into a cricket sitting on the tree.
The Four Seasons go on for ever and ever:
In all Nature nothing stops to rest
Even for a moment. Only the sick man's heart
Deep down still aches as of old!

[1] The epidendrum.

154

At the End of Spring

To Yüan Chēn.[1] (A. D. 810)

The flower of the pear-tree gathers and turns to fruit;
The swallows' eggs have hatched into young birds.
When the Seasons' changes thus confront the mind
What comfort can the Doctrine of Tao give?
It will teach me to watch the days and months fly
Without grieving that Youth slips away;
If the Fleeting World is but a long dream,
It does not matter whether one is young or old.
But ever since the day that my friend left my side
And has lived an exile in the City of Chiang-ling,
There is one wish I cannot quite destroy:
That from time to time we may chance to meet again.

[1] Po Chū-i's great friend. See pages 259 and 270.

The Poem on the Wall

(A.D. 810)

*[Yüan Chēn wrote that on his way to exile he had discovered
a poem inscribed by Po Chü-i, on the wall of the Lo-k'ou Inn.]*

My clumsy poem on the inn-wall none cared to see.
With bird-droppings and moss's growth the letters were
    blotched away.
There came a guest with heart so full, that though a page
    to the Throne,
He did not grudge with his broidered coat to wipe off the
    dust, and read.

156

Chu-ch'ēn Village

(A.D. 811)

In Hsü-chou, in the District of Ku-fēng
There lies a village whose name is Chu-ch'ēn—
A hundred miles away from the county-town,
Amid fields of hemp and green of mulberry-trees.
Click, click goes the sound of the spinning-wheel;
Mules and oxen pack the village-streets.
The girls go drawing the water from the brook;
The men go gathering fire-wood on the hill.
So far from the town Government affairs are few;
So deep in the hills, man's ways are simple.
Though they have wealth, they do not traffic with it;
Though they reach the age, they do not enter the Army.
Each family keeps to its village trade;
Grey-headed, they have never left the gates.

Alive, they are the people of Ch'ēn Village;
Dead, they become the dust of Ch'ēn Village.
Out in the fields old men and young
Gaze gladly, each in the other's face.
In the whole village there are only two clans;
Age after age Chus have married Ch'ēns.
Near or distant, they have kinsmen in every house;
Young or old, they have friends wherever they go.

On white wine and roasted fowl they fare
At joyful meetings more than "once a week".
While they are alive, they have no distant partings;
To choose a wife they go to a neighbour's house.
When they are dead,—no distant burial;
Round the village graves lie thick.
They are not troubled either about life or death;
They have no anguish either of body or soul.
And so it happens that they live to a ripe age
And great-great-grandsons are often seen.

I was born in the Realms of Etiquette;
In early years, unprotected and poor.
Alone, I learnt to distinguish between Evil and Good;
Untutored, I toiled at bitter tasks.
The World's Law honours Learning and Fame;
Scholars prize marriages and Caps.
With these fetters I gyved my own hands;
Truly I became a much-deceived man.
At ten years old I learnt to read books;
At fifteen, I knew how to write prose.
At twenty I was made a Bachelor of Arts;
At thirty I became a Censor at the Court.
Above, the duty I owe to Prince and parents;
Below, the ties that bind me to wife and child.
The support of my family, the service of my country—
For these tasks my nature is not apt.
I reckon the time that I first left my home;

From then till now,—fifteen Springs!
My lonely boat has thrice sailed to Ch'u;
Four times through Ch'in my lean horse has passed.
I have walked in the morning with hunger in my face;
I have lain at night with a soul that could not rest.
East and West I have wandered without pause,
Hither and thither like a cloud astray in the sky.
In the civil-war my old home was destroyed;
Of my flesh and blood many are scattered and lost.
    North of the River, and South of the River—
In both lands are the friends of all my life;
Life-friends whom I never see at all,—
Whose deaths I hear of only after the lapse of years.
Sad at morning, I lie on my bed till dusk;
Weeping at night, I sit and wait for dawn.
The fire of sorrow has burnt my heart's core;
The frost of trouble has seized my hair's roots.
In such anguish has my whole life passed;
Long I have envied the people of Ch'ēn Village.

Fishing in the Wei River

(A. D. 811)

In waters still as a burnished mirror's face,
In the depths of Wei, carp and grayling swim.
Idly I come with my bamboo fishing-rod
And hang my hook by the banks of Wei stream.
A gentle wind blows on my fishing-gear
Softly shaking my ten feet of line.
Though my body sits waiting for fish to come,
My heart has wandered to the Land of Nothingness.[1]
Long ago a white-headed man[2]
Also fished at the same river's side;
A hooker of men, not a hooker of fish,
At seventy years, he caught Wēn Wang.[2]
But I, when I come to cast my hook in the stream,
Have no thought either of fish or men.
Lacking the skill to capture either prey,
I can only bask in the autumn water's light.
When I tire of this, my fishing also stops;
I go to my home and drink my cup of wine.

[1] See "Chuang Tzŭ", chap. i, end.
[2] The Sage T'ai-kung sat still till he was seventy, apparently fishing, but really waiting for a Prince who would employ him. At last Wēn Wang, Prince of Chou, happened to come that way and at once made him his counsellor.

160

Illness and Idleness

(Circa A.D. 812)

Illness and idleness give me much leisure.
What do I do with my leisure, when it comes?
I cannot bring myself to discard inkstone and brush;
Now and then I make a new poem.
When the poem is made, it is slight and flavourless,
A thing of derision to almost every one.
Superior people will be pained at the flatness or the metre;
Common people will hate the plainness of the words.
I sing it to myself, then stop and think about it . . .

The Prefects of Soochow and P'ēng-tsē[1]
Would perhaps have praised it, but they died long ago.
    Who else would care to hear it?
No one to-day except Yüan Chēn,
And *he* is banished to the City of Chiang-ling,
For three years an usher in the Penal Court.
Parted from me by three thousand leagues
He will never know even that the poem was made.

[1] Wei Ying-wu, eighth century A.D., and T'ao Ch'ien, A.D. 372-427.

The Chrysanthemums
in the Eastern Garden

(A.D. 812)

The days of my youth left me long ago;
And now in their turn dwindle my years of prime.
With what thoughts of sadness and loneliness
I walk again in this cold, deserted place!
In the midst of the garden long I stand alone;
The sunshine, faint; the wind and dew chill.

The autumn lettuce is tangled and turned to seed;
The fair trees are blighted and withered away.
All that is left are a few chrysanthemum-flowers
That have newly opened beneath the wattled fence.
I had brought wine and meant to fill my cup,
When the sight of these made me stay my hand.
        I remember, when I was young,
How easily my mood changed from sad to gay.
If I saw wine, no matter at what season,
Before I drank it, my heart was already glad.
        But now that age comes,
A moment of joy is harder and harder to get.
And always I fear that when I am quite old
The strongest liquor will leave me comfortless.
Therefore I ask you, late chrysanthemum-flower
At this sad season why do you bloom alone?
Though well I know that it was not for my sake,
Taught by you, for a while I will open my face.

Winter Night

(Written during his retirement in A. D. 812)

My house is poor; those that I love have left me;
My body is sick; I cannot join the feast.
There is not a living soul before my eyes
As I lie alone locked in my cottage room.
My broken lamp burns with a feeble flame;
My tattered curtains are crooked and do not meet.
"Tsek, tsek" on the door-step and window-sill
Again I hear the new snow fall.
As I grow older, gradually I sleep less;
I wake at midnight and sit up straight in bed.
If I had not learned the "art of sitting and forgetting",[1]
How could I bear this utter loneliness?
Stiff and stark my body cleaves to the earth;
Unimpeded my soul yields to Change.[2]
So has it been for four hateful years,
Through one thousand and three hundred nights!

[1] Yen Hui told Confucius that he had acquired the "art of sitting and forgetting". Asked what that meant, Yen Hui replied, "I have learnt to discard my body and obliterate my intelligence; to abandon matter and be impervious to sense-perception. By this method I become one with the All-Pervading".—*Chuang Tzŭ*, chap. vi.
[2] "Change", the principle of endless mutation which governs the Universe.

Poems in Depression, at Wei Village

(A.D. 812)

[1]

I hug my pillow and do not speak a word;
In my empty room no sound stirs.
Who knows that, all day a-bed,
I am not ill and am not even asleep?

[2]

Turned to jade are the boy's rosy cheeks;
To his sick temples the frost of winter clings. . . .
Do not wonder that my body sinks to decay;
Though my limbs are old, my heart is older yet.

The Dragon of the Black Pool

[*A Satire*]

Deep the waters of the Black Pool, coloured like ink;
They say a Holy Dragon lives there, whom men have
    never seen.
Beside the Pool they have built a shrine; the authorities
    have established a ritual;
A dragon by itself remains a dragon, but men can make
    it a god.
Prosperity and disaster, rain and drought, plagues and
    pestilences—
By the village people were all regarded as the Sacred
    Dragon's doing.
They all made offerings of sucking-pig and poured libations
    of wine;
The morning prayers and evening gifts depended on
    a "medium's" advice.

When the dragon comes, ah!
The wind stirs and sighs
Paper money thrown, ah!
Silk umbrellas waved.
When the dragon goes, ah!
The wind also—still.
Incense-fire dies, ah!
The cups and vessels are cold.[1]
Meats lie stacked on the rocks of the Pool's shore;
Wine flows on the grass in front of the shrine.
I do not know, of all those offerings, how much the
    Dragon eats;
But the mice of the woods and the foxes of the hills are
    continually drunk and sated.
        Why are the foxes so lucky?
        What have the sucking-pigs done,
That year by year *they* should be killed, merely to glut
    the foxes?
That the foxes are robbing the Sacred Dragon and eating
    His sucking-pig,
Beneath the nine-fold depths of His pool, does He know
    or not?

[1] Parody of a famous Han dynasty hymn.

The People of Tao-chou

In the land of Tao-chou
Many of the people are dwarfs;
The tallest of them never grow to more than three feet.
They were sold in the market as dwarf slaves and yearly
    sent to Court;
Described as "an offering of natural products from the land
    of Tao-chou".
A strange "offering of natural products"; I never heard of
    one yet
That parted men from those they loved, never to meet again!
Old men—weeping for their grandsons; mothers for their
    children!
One day—Yang Ch'ēng came to govern the land;
He refused to send up dwarf slaves in spite of incessant
    mandates.
He replied to the Emperor "Your servant finds in the Six
    Canonical Books
'In offering products, one must offer what is there, and not
    what isn't there'
On the waters and lands of Tao-chou, among all the things
    that live
I only find dwarfish *people*; no dwarfish *slaves*".

168

The Emperor's heart was deeply moved and he sealed and
    sent a scroll
"The yearly tribute of dwarfish slaves is henceforth
    annulled."
              The people of Tao-chou,
Old ones and young ones, how great their joy!
Father with son and brother with brother henceforward
    kept together;
From that day for ever more they lived as free men.
              The people of Tao-chou
              Still enjoy this gift.
And even now when they speak of the Governor
Tears start to their eyes.
And lest their children and their children's children should
    forget the Governor's name,
When boys are born the syllable "Yang" is often used in
    their forename.

The Grain-Tribute

Written circa A. D. 812, showing one of the poet's periods of retirement. When the officials come to receive his grain-tribute, he remembers that he is only giving back what he had taken during his years of office. Salaries were paid partly in kind.

There came an officer knocking by night at my door—
In a loud voice demanding grain-tribute.
My house-servants dared not wait till the morning,
But brought candles and set them on the barn-floor.
Passed through the sieve, clean-washed as pearls,
A whole cart-load, thirty bushels of grain.
But still they cry that it is not paid in full:
With whips and curses they goad my servants and boys.
Once, in error, I entered public life;
I am inwardly ashamed that my talents were not sufficient.
In succession I occupied four official posts;
For doing nothing,—ten years' salary!
Often have I heard that saying of ancient men
That "good and ill follow in an endless chain".
And to-day it ought to set my heart at rest
To return to others the corn in my great barn.

170

The Old Harp

Of cord and cassia-wood is the harp compounded:
Within it lie ancient melodies.
Ancient melodies—weak and savourless,
Not appealing to present men's taste.
Light and colour are faded from the jade stops:
Dust has covered the rose-red strings.
Decay and ruin came to it long ago,
But the sound that is left is still cold and clear.
I do not refuse to play it, if you want me to:
But even if I play, people will not listen.

How did it come to be neglected so?
Because of the Ch'iang flute and the Ch'in flageolet.[1]

[1] Barbarous modern instruments.

The Harper of Chao

The singers have hushed their notes of clear song:
The red sleeves of the dancers are motionless.
Hugging his lute, the old harper of Chao
Rocks and sways as he touches the five chords.
The loud notes swell and scatter abroad:
"Sa, sa," like wind blowing the rain.
The soft notes dying almost to nothing:
"Ch'ieh, ch'ieh", like the voice of ghosts talking.
Now as glad as the magpie's lucky song:
Again bitter as the gibbon's ominous cry.
His ten fingers have no fixed note:
Up and down—*kung, chih,* and *yü.*[1]
And those who sit and listen to the tune he plays
Of soul and body lose the mastery.
And those who pass that way as he plays the tune,
Suddenly stop and cannot raise their feet.

Alas, alas that the ears of common men
Should love the modern and not love the old.
Thus it is that the harp in the green window
Day by day is covered deeper with dust.

[1] Tonic, dominant and superdominant of the ancient five-note scale.

172

The Flower Market

In the Royal City spring is almost over:
Tinkle, tinkle—the coaches and horsemen pass.
We tell each other "This is the peony season":
And follow with the crowd that goes to the Flower Market.
"Cheap and dear—no uniform price:
The cost of the plant depends on the number of blossoms.
For the fine flower,—a hundred pieces of damask:
For the cheap flower,—five bits of silk.
Above is spread an awning to protect them:
Around is woven a wattle-fence to screen them.
If you sprinkle water and cover the roots with mud,
When they are transplanted, they will not lose their beauty."
Each household thoughtlessly follows the custom,
Man by man, no one realizing.
There happened to be an old farm labourer
            Who came by chance that way.
He bowed his head and sighed a deep sigh:
But this sigh nobody understood.
He was thinking, "A cluster of deep-red flowers
Would pay the taxes of ten poor houses".

The Prisoner

(Written in A.D. 809)

Tartars led in chains,
Tartars led in chains!
Their ears pierced, their faces bruised—they are driven into
the land of Ch'in.
The Son of Heaven took pity on them and would not have
them slain.
He sent them away to the south-east, to the lands of Wu
and Yüeh.
A petty officer in a yellow coat took down their names
and surnames.
They were led from the city of Ch'ang-an under escort of
an armed guard.
Their bodies were covered with the wounds of arrows,
their bones stood out from their cheeks.
They had grown so weak they could only march a single
stage a day.
In the morning they must satisfy hunger and thirst with
neither plate nor cup:
At night they must lie in their dirt and rags on beds that
stank with filth.
Suddenly they came to the Yangtze River and remembered
the waters of Chiao.[1]

[1] In Turkestan.

174

With lowered hands and levelled voices they sobbed a
    muffled song.
Then one Tartar lifted up his voice and spoke to the
    other Tartars,
"*Your* sorrows are none at all compared with *my* sorrows."
Those that were with him in the same band asked to hear
    his tale:
  As he tried to speak the words were choked by anger.
He told them "I was born and bred in the town of
    Liang-yüan.[1]
In the frontier wars of Ta-li[2] I fell into the Tartars' hands.
Since the days the Tartars took me alive forty years
    have passed:
They put me into a coat of skins tied with a belt of rope.
Only on the first of the first month might I wear my
    Chinese dress.
As I put on my coat and arranged my cap, how fast the
    tears flowed!
I made in my heart a secret vow I would find a way home:
I hid my plan from my Tartar wife and the children she had
    borne me in the land.
I thought to myself, 'It is well for me that my limbs are
    still strong',
And yet, being old, in my heart I feared I should never live
    to return.

[1] North of Ch'ang-an.
[2] The period Ta-li, A. D. 766-780.

175

The Tartar chieftains shoot so well that the birds are afraid
     to fly:
From the risk of their arrows I escaped alive and fled
     swiftly home.
Hiding all day and walking all night, I crossed the Great
     Desert.[1]
Where clouds are dark and the moon black and the sands
     eddy in the wind.
Frightened, I sheltered at the Green Grave,[2] where the
     frozen grasses are few:
Stealthily I crossed the Yellow River, at night, on the
     thin ice,
Suddenly I heard Han[3] drums and the sound of
     soldiers coming:
I went to meet them at the road-side, bowing to them as
     they came.
But the moving horsemen did not hear that I spoke the
     Han tongue:
Their Captain took me for a Tartar born and had me bound
     in chains.
They are sending me away to the south-east, to a low and
     swampy land:
No one now will take pity on me: resistance is all in vain.

[1] The Gobi Desert.
[2] The grave of Chao-chün, a Chinese girl who in 33 B. c. was "bestowed
upon the Khan of the Hsiung-nu as a mark of Imperial regard" [Giles].
Hers was the only grave in this desolate district on which grass would
grow.   [3] I.e., Chinese.

Thinking of this, my voice chokes and I ask of
    Heaven above,
Was I spared from death only to spend the rest of my years
    in sorrow?
My native village of Liang-yüan I shall not see again:
My wife and children in the Tartars' land I have
    fruitlessly deserted.
When I fell among Tartars and was taken prisoner, I pined
    for the land of Han:
Now that I am back in the land of Han, they have turned
    me into a Tartar.
Had I but known what my fate would be, I would not
    have started home!
For the two lands, so wide apart, are alike in the sorrow
    they bring.
        Tartar prisoners in chains!
Of all the sorrows of all the prisoners mine is the hardest
    to bear!
Never in the world has so great a wrong befallen the lot
    of man,—
A Han heart and a Han tongue set in the body of a Turk".

The Chancellor's Gravel-Drive

[A Satire on the Maltreatment of Subordinates]

A Government-bull yoked to a Government-cart!
Moored by the bank of Ch'an River, a barge loaded
    with gravel.
A single load of gravel,
How many pounds it weighs!
Carrying at dawn, carrying at dusk, what is it all for?
They are carrying it towards the Five Gates,
To the West of the Main Road.
Under the shadow of green laurels they are making a
    gravel-drive.
For yesterday arrove, newly appointed,
The Assistant Chancellor of the Realm,
And was terribly afraid that the wet and mud
Would dirty his horse's hoofs.
The Chancellor's horse's hoofs
Stepped on the gravel and remained perfectly clean;
But the bull employed in dragging the cart
Was almost sweating blood.
The Assistant Chancellor's business
Is to "save men, govern the country
And harmonize Yin and Yang."[1]
Whether the bull's neck is sore
Need not trouble him at all.

---

[1] The negative and positive principles in nature.

178

The Man Who Dreamed of Fairies

This poem is an attack on the Emperor Hsien-tsung, A. D. 806-820, who "was devoted to magic". A Taoist wizard told him that herbs of longevity grew near the city of T'ai-chou. The Emperor at once appointed him prefect of the place, "pour lui permettre d'herboriser plus à son aise" (Wieger, Textes III, p. 1723). When the censors protested, the Emperor replied: "The ruin of a single district would be a small price to pay, if it could procure longevity for the Lord of Men."

There was once a man who dreamt he went to Heaven:
His dream-body soared aloft through space.
He rode on the back of a white-plumed crane,
And was led on his flight by two crimson banners.
Whirring of wings and flapping of coat tails!
Jade bells suddenly all a-tinkle!
Half way to Heaven, he looked down beneath him,
Down on the dark turmoil of the World.
Gradually he lost the place of his native town;
Mountains and water—nothing else distinct.
The Eastern Ocean—a single strip of white:
The Hills of China,—five specks of green.
Gliding past him a host of fairies swept
In long procession to the Palace of the Jade City.

179

How should he guess that the children of Tzŭ-mēn[1]
Bow to the throne like courtiers of earthly kings?
They take him to the presence of the Mighty Jade Emperor:
He bows his head and proffers loyal homage.
The Emperor says: "We see you have fairy talents:
Be of good heart and do not slight yourself.
We shall send to fetch you in fifteen years
And give you a place in the Courtyard of Immortality."
Twice bowing, he acknowledged the gracious words:
Then woke from sleep, full of wonder and joy.
He hid his secret and dared not tell it abroad:
But vowed a vow he would live in a cave of rock.
From love and affection he severed kith and kin:
From his eating and drinking he omitted savoury and spice.
His morning meal was a dish of coral-dust:
At night he sipped an essence of dewy mists.
In the empty mountains he lived for thirty years
Daily watching for the Heavenly Coach to come.
The time of appointment was already long past,
But of wings and coach-bells—still no sound.
His teeth and hair daily withered and decayed:
His ears and eyes gradually lost their keenness.
One morning he suffered the Common Change
And his body was one with the dust and dirt of the hill.
Gods and fairies! If indeed such things there be,
Their ways are beyond the striving of mortal men.
If you have not on your skull the Golden Bump's protrusion,

[1] I.e., the Immortals.

180

If your name is absent from the rolls of the Red Terrace,
In vain you learn the "Method of Avoiding Food":
For naught you study the "Book of Alchemic Lore".
Though you sweat and toil, what shall your trouble bring?
You will only shorten the five-score years of your span.
Sad, alas, the man who dreamt of Fairies!
For a single dream spoiled his whole life.

Magic

Boundless, the great sea.
Straight down,—no bottom: sideways,—no border.
Of cloudy waves and misty billows down in the uttermost
    depths
Men have fabled, in the midst there stand three sacred hills.
On the hills, thick growing,—herbs that banish Death.
Wings grow on those who eat them and they turn into
    heavenly "hsien".
The Lord of Ch'in[1] and Wu of Han[2] believed in these
    stories:
And magic-workers year by year were sent to gather the
    herbs.
The Blessed Islands, now and of old, what but an empty
    tale?
The misty waters spread before them and they knew not
    where to seek.
            Boundless, the great sea.
            Dauntless, the mighty wind.
Their eyes search but cannot see the shores of the
    Blessed Islands.

[1] The "First Emperor", 259-210 B. C.
[2] Wu Ti, 156-87 B. C.

182

They cannot find the Blessed Isles and yet they dare
    not return:
Youths and maidens that began the quest grew grey on
    board the boat.
They found that the writings of Hsü Fu[1] were all boasts
    and lies:
To the Lofty Principle and Great Unity in vain they raised
    their prayers.
                Do you not see
The graves on the top of Black Horse Hill[2] and the tombs
    at Mo-ling?[3]
What is left but the sighing wind blowing in the
    tangled grasses?
                Yes, and what is more,
The Dark and Primal Master of Sages in his five
    thousand words[4]
                Never spoke of herbs,
                Never spoke of "hsien",
Nor spoke of soaring in broad daylight up to the
    blue heaven.

---

[1] = Hsü Shih. Giles, 1276.
[2] The burial-places of these two Emperors.   [3] *Ibid.*
[4] Lao-tzü, in the Tao Tē Ching.

The Two Red Towers

[*A Satire Against Clericalism*]

The Two Red Towers
North and south rise facing each other.
I beg to ask, to whom do they belong?
To the two Princes of the period Chēng Yüan.[1]
The two Princes blew on their flutes and drew down fairies
    from the sky.
Who carried them off through the Five Clouds, soaring
    away to Heaven.
Their halls and houses, that they could take with them,
Were turned into Temples planted in the Dust of the World.
In the tiring-rooms and dancers' towers all is silent and still;
Only the willows like dancers' arms, and the pond
    like a mirror.
When the flowers are falling at yellow twilight, when things
    are sad and hushed,
One does not hear songs and flutes, but only chimes
    and bells.
The Imperial Patent on the Temple doors is written in letters
    of gold;
For nuns' quarters and monks' cells ample space is allowed.

[1] A. D. 785-805.

184

For green moss and bright moonlight—plenty of room
    provided;
In a hovel opposite is a sick man who has hardly room to
    lie down.
I remember once when at P'ing-yang they were building a
    great man's house
How it swallowed up the housing space of thousands of
    ordinary men.
The Immortals[1] are leaving us, two by two, and their houses
    are turned into Temples;
I begin to fear that the whole world will become
    a vast convent.

[1] Hsien Tsung's brothers?

The Charcoal-Seller

[A Satire Against "Kommandatur"]

An old charcoal-seller
Cutting wood and burning charcoal in the forest of the
  Southern Mountain.
His face, stained with dust and ashes, has turned to the colour
  of smoke.
The hair on his temples is streaked with gray: his ten fingers
  are black.
The money he gets by selling charcoal, how far does it go?
It is just enough to clothe his limbs and put food in his mouth.
Although, alas, the coat on his back is a coat without lining,
He hopes for the coming of cold weather, to send up the
  price of coal!
Last night, outside the city,—a whole foot of snow;
At dawn he drives the charcoal wagon along the frozen ruts.
Oxen,—weary; man,—hungry: the sun, already high;
Outside the Gate, to the south of the Market, at last they stop
  in the mud.
Suddenly, a pair of prancing horsemen. Who can it
  be coming?
A public official in a yellow coat and a boy in a white shirt.

186

In their hands they hold a written warrant: on their tongues
     —the words of an order;
They turn back the wagon and curse the oxen, leading them
     off to the north.
A whole wagon of charcoal,
More than a thousand pieces!
If officials choose to take it away, the woodman may
     not complain.
Half a piece of red silk and a single yard of damask,
The Courtiers have tied to the oxen's collar, as the price
     of a wagon of coal!

The Politician

I was going to the City to sell the herbs I had plucked;
On the way I rested by some trees at the Blue Gate.
Along the road there came a horseman riding;
Whose face was pale with a strange look of dread.
Friends and relations, waiting to say good-bye,
Pressed at his side, but he did not dare to pause.
I, in wonder, asked the people about me
Who he was and what had happened to him.
They told me this was a Privy Councillor
Whose grave duties were like the pivot of State.
His food allowance was ten thousand cash;
Three times a day the Emperor came to his house.
Yesterday he was called to a meeting of Heroes:
To-day he is banished to the country of Yai-chou.
So always, the Counsellors of Kings;
Favour and ruin changed between dawn and dusk!
Green, green,—the grass of the Eastern Suburb;
And amid the grass, a road that leads to the hills.
Resting in peace among the white clouds,
At last he has made a "coup" that cannot fail!

The Old Man with the Broken Arm

[*A Satire on Militarism*]

At Hsin-fēng an old man—four-score and eight;

The hair on his head and the hair of his eyebrows—white as
the new snow.

Leaning on the shoulders of his great-grandchildren, he walks
in front of the Inn;

With his left arm he leans on their shoulders; his right arm is
broken.

I asked the old man how many years had passed since he
broke his arm;

I also asked the cause of the injury, how and why it
happened?

The old man said he was born and reared in the District
of Hsin-fēng;

At the time of his birth—a wise reign; no wars or discords.

"Often I listened in the Pear-Tree Garden to the sound of
flute and song;

Naught I knew of banner and lance; nothing of arrow
or bow.

Then came the wars of T'ien-pao[1] and the great levy of men;

Of three men in each house,—one man was taken.

[1] A.D. 742-755.

And those to whom the lot fell, where were they taken to?
Five months' journey, a thousand miles—away to Yün-nan.
We heard it said that in Yün-nan there flows the Lu River;
As the flowers fall from the pepper-trees, poisonous vapours
　　rise.
When the great army waded across, the water seethed like
　　a cauldron;
When barely ten had entered the water, two or three
　　were dead.
To the north of my village, to the south of my village the
　　sound of weeping and wailing,
Children parting from fathers and mothers; husbands parting
　　from wives.
Everyone says that in expeditions against the Min tribes
Of a million men who are sent out, not one returns.
　　　　　I, that am old, was then twenty-four;
My name and fore-name were written down in the rolls
　　of the Board of War.
In the depth of the night not daring to let any one know
I secretly took a huge stone and dashed it against my arm.
For drawing the bow and waving the banner now
　　wholly unfit;
I knew henceforward I should not be sent to fight in Yün-nan.
Bones broken and sinews wounded could not fail to hurt;
I was ready enough to bear pain, if only I got back home.
My arm—broken ever since; it was sixty years ago.
One limb, although destroyed,—whole body safe!

But even now on winter nights when the wind and rain blow
From evening on till day's dawn I cannot sleep for pain.
       Not sleeping for pain
        Is a small thing to bear,
Compared with the joy of being alive when all the rest
   are dead.
For otherwise, years ago, at the ford of Lu River

My body would have died and my soul hovered by the bones
    that no one gathered.
A ghost, I'd have wandered in Yün-nan, always looking
    for home.
Over the graves of ten thousand soldiers, mournfully
    hovering."
              So the old man spoke,
          And I bid you listen to his words
            Have you not heard
That the Prime Minister of K'ai-yüan,[1] Sung K'ai-fu,
Did not reward frontier exploits, lest a spirit of aggression
    should prevail?
            And have you not heard
That the Prime Minister of T'ien-Pao, Yang Kuo-chung[2]
Desiring to win imperial favour, started a frontier war?
But long before he could win the war, people had lost
    their temper;
Ask the man with the broken arm in the village of Hsin-fēng!

[1] A. D. 713-742.
[2] Cousin of the notorious mistress of Ming-huang, Yang Kuei-fei.

192

Kept Waiting in the Boat at Chiu-k'ou Ten Days by an Adverse Wind

White billows and huge waves block the river crossing;
Wherever I go, danger and difficulty; whatever I do, failure.
Just as in my worldly career I wander and lose the road,
So when I come to the river crossing, I am stopped by
    contrary winds.
Of fishes and prawns sodden in the rain the smell fills my
    nostrils;
With the stings of insects that come with the fog, my whole
    body is sore.
I am growing old, time flies, and my short span runs out,
While I sit in a boat at Chiu-k'ou, wasting ten days!

Arriving at Hsün-yang

Two Poems

[1]

A bend of the river brings into view two triumphal arches;
That is the gate in the western wall of the suburbs of
    Hsün-yang.
I have still to travel in my solitary boat three or four
    leagues—
By misty waters and rainy sands, while the yellow
    dusk thickens.

[2]

We are almost come to Hsün-yang: how my thoughts
    are stirred
As we pass to the south of Yü Liang's[1] tower and the east
    of P'ên Port.
The forest trees are leafless and withered,—after the
    mountain rain;
The roofs of the houses are hidden low among the
    river mists.
The horses, fed on water grass, are too weak to carry
    their load;
The cottage walls of wattle and thatch let the wind blow
    on one's bed.
In the distance I see red-wheeled coaches driving from the
    town-gate;
They have taken the trouble, these civil people, to meet
    their new Prefect!

[1] Died A. D. 340. Giles, 2526.

On Board Ship:
Reading Yüan Chēn's Poems

I take your poems in my hand and read them beside
    the candle;
The poems are finished: the candle is low: dawn not
    yet come.
With sore eyes by the guttering candle still I sit in the dark,
Listening to waves that, driven by the wind, strike the prow
    of the ship.

Madly Singing in the Mountains

There is no one among men that has not a special failing:
And my failing consists in writing verses.
I have broken away from the thousand ties of life:
But this infirmity still remains behind.
Each time that I look at a fine landscape:
Each time that I meet a loved friend,
I raise my voice and recite a stanza of poetry
And am glad as though a God had crossed my path.
Ever since the day I was banished to Hsün-yang
Half my time I have lived among the hills.
And often, when I have finished a new poem,
Alone I climb the road to the Eastern Rock.
I lean my body on the banks of white stone:
I pull down with my hands a green cassia branch.
My mad singing startles the valleys and hills:
The apes and birds all come to peep.
Fearing to become a laughing-stock to the world,
I choose a place that is unfrequented by men.

Releasing a Migrant "Yen"
(Wild Goose)

At Nine Rivers,[1] in the tenth year,[2] in winter,—heavy snow;
The river-water covered with ice and the forests broken
    with their load.[3]
The birds of the air, hungry and cold, went flying
    east and west;
And with them flew a migrant "yen" loudly clamouring
    for food.
Among the snow it pecked for grass; and rested on the
    surface of the ice:
It tried with its wings to scale the sky; but its tired flight
    was slow.
The boys of the river spread a net and caught the bird
    as it flew;
They took it in their hands to the city-market and sold it
    there alive.
I that was once a man of the North am now an exile here:
Bird and man, in their different kind, are each strangers
    in the south.

[1] Kiukiang, the poet's place of exile.
[2] A. D. 815. His first winter at Kiukiang.
[3] By the weight of snow.

198

And because the sight of an exiled bird wounded an
    exile's heart,
I paid your ransom and set you free, and you flew away to
    the clouds.
Yen, Yen, flying to the clouds, tell me, whither shall you go?
Of all things I bid you, do not fly to the land of the
    north-west;
In Huai-hsi there are rebel bands[1] that have not been
    subdued;
And a thousand thousand armoured men have long been
    camped in war.
The official army and the rebel army have grown old in
    their opposite trenches;
The soldier's rations have grown so small, they'll be glad
    of even you.
The brave boys, in their hungry plight, will shoot you and
    eat your flesh;
They will pluck from your body those long feathers and
    make them into arrow-wings!

[1] The revolt of Wu Yüan-chi.

199

To His Brother Hsing-chien, who was Serving in Tung-ch'uan

(A. D. 815)

Sullen, sullen, my brows are ever knit;
Silent, silent, my lips will not move.
It is not indeed that I choose to sorrow thus;
If I lift my eyes, who would share my joy?
Last Spring *you* were called to the West
To carry arms in the lands of Pa and Shu;
And this Spring I was banished to the South
To nurse my sickness on the River's oozy banks.
You are parted from me by six thousand leagues;
In another world, under another sky.
Of ten letters, nine do not reach;
What can I do to open my sad face?
Thirsty men often dream of drink;
Hungry men often dream of food.
Since Spring came, where do my dreams lodge?
Ere my eyes are closed, I have travelled to Tung-ch'uan.

Starting Early from the Ch'u-ch'ēng Inn

(A. D. 815)

Washed by the rain, dust and grime are laid;
Skirting the river, the road's course is flat.
The moon has risen on the last remnants of night;
The travellers' speed profits by the early cold.
In the great silence I whisper a faint song;
In the black darkness are bred sombre thoughts.
On the lotus-banks hovers a dewy breeze;
Through the rice-furrows trickles a singing stream.
At the noise of our bells a sleeping dog stirs;
At the sight of our torches a roosting bird wakes.
Dawn glimmers through the shapes of misty trees . . .
For ten miles, till day at last breaks.

Rain

(A. D. 815)

Since I lived a stranger in the City of Hsün-yang
Hour by hour bitter rain has poured.
On few days has the dark sky cleared;
In listless sleep I have spent much time.
The lake has widened till it almost joins the sky;
The clouds sink till they touch the water's face.
Beyond my hedge I hear the boatmen's talk;
At the street-end I hear the fisher's song.
Misty birds are lost in yellow air;
Windy sails kick the white waves.
In front of my gate the horse and carriage-way
In a single night has turned into a river-bed.

202

The Beginning of Summer

(A.D. 815)

At the rise of summer a hundred beasts and trees
Join in gladness that the Season bids them thrive.
Stags and does frolic in the deep woods;
Snakes and insects are pleased by the rank grass.
Wingèd birds love the thick leaves;
Scaly fish enjoy the fresh weeds.
But to one place Summer forgot to come;
I alone am left like a withered straw . . .
     Banished to the world's end;
Flesh and bone all in distant ways.
From my native-place no tidings come;
Rebel troops flood the land with war.
Sullen grief, in the end, what will it bring?
I am only wearing my own heart away.
Better far to let both body and mind
Blindly yield to the fate that Heaven made.
Hsün-yang abounds in good wine;
I will fill my cup and never let it be dry.
On Pēn River fish are cheap as mud;
Early and late I will eat them, boiled and fried.
With morning rice at the temple under the hill,
And evening wine at the island in the lake . . .
Why should my thoughts turn to my native land?
For in this place one could well end one's age.

Visiting the Hsi-lin Temple

(Written during his exile)

I dismount from my horse at the Hsi-lin Temple;
I throw the porter my slender riding-whip.
In the morning I work at a Government office-desk;
In the evening I become a dweller in the Sacred Hills.
In the second month to the north of Kuang-lu
The ice breaks and the snow begins to melt.
On the southern plantation the tea-plant thrusts its sprouts;
Through the northern sluice the veins of the spring ooze.

This year there is war in An-hui,
In every place soldiers are rushing to arms.
Men of learning have been summoned to the Council Board;
Men of action are marching to the battle-line.
Only I, who have no talents at all,
Am left in the mountains to play with the pebbles of
    the stream.

204

Hearing the Early Oriole

(Written in exile)

When the sun rose I was still lying in bed;
An early oriole sang on the roof of my house.
For a moment I thought of the Royal Park at dawn
When the Birds of Spring greeted their Lord from his trees.
I remembered the days when I served before the Throne
Pencil in hand, on duty at the Ch'ēng-ming;[1]
At the height of spring, when I paused an instant from work,
Morning and evening, was *this* the voice I heard?
Now in my exile the oriole sings again
In the dreary stillness of Hsün-yang town . . .
The bird's note cannot really have changed;
All the difference lies in the listener's heart.
If he could but forget that he lives at the World's end,
The bird would sing as it sang in the Palace of old.

[1] Name of a palace at Ch'ang-an.

Dreaming that I went with Lu and Yu to visit Yüan Chēn

(Written in exile)

At night I dreamt I was back in Ch'ang-an;
I saw again the faces of old friends.
And in my dreams, under an April sky,
They led me by the hand to wander in the spring winds.
Together we came to the village of Peace and Quiet;
We stopped our horses at the gate of Yüan Chēn.
Yüan Chēn was sitting all alone;
When he saw me coming, a smile came to his face.
He pointed back at the flowers in the western court;
Then opened wine in the northern summer-house.
He seemed to be saying that neither of us had changed;
He seemed to be regretting that joy will not stay;
That our souls had met only for a little while,
To part again with hardly time for greeting.
I woke up and thought him still at my side;
I put out my hand; there was nothing there at all.

206

To a Portrait Painter
who desired Him to Sit

You, so bravely splashing reds and blues!
Just when *I* am getting wrinkled and old.
Why should you waste the moments of inspiration
Tracing the withered limbs of a sick man?
Tall, tall is the Palace of Ch'i-lin;[1]
But my deeds have not been frescoed on its walls.
Minutely limned on a foot of painting silk—
What can I do with a portrait such as *that*?

[1] One of the "Record Offices" of the T'ang dynasty, where meritorious deeds were illustrated on the walls.

Separation

Yesterday I heard that such-a-one was gone;
This morning they tell me that so-and-so is dead.
Of friends and acquaintances more than two-thirds
Have suffered change and passed to the Land of Ghosts.
Those that are gone I shall not see again;
They, alas, are for ever finished and done.
Those that are left,—where are they now?
They are all scattered,—a thousand miles away.
Those I have known and loved through all my life,
On the fingers of my hand—how many do I count?
Only the prefects of T'ung, Kuo and Li
And Fēng Province—just those four.[1]
Longing for each other we are all grown gray;
Through the Fleeting World rolled like a wave in
      the stream.
Alas that the feasts and frolics of old days
Have withered and vanished, bringing us to this!
When shall we meet and drink a cup of wine
And laughing gaze into each other's eyes?

---

[1] Yūan Chēn [d. 831], Ts'ui Hsüan-liang [d. 833], Liu Yū-hsi [d. 842], and Li Chien [d. 821].

The Red Cockatoo

Sent as a present from Annam—
A red cockatoo.
Coloured like the peach-tree blossom,
Speaking with the speech of men.
And they did to it what is always done
To the learned and eloquent.
They took a cage with stout bars
And shut it up inside.

Eating Bamboo-Shoots

My new province is a land of bamboo-groves:
Their shoots in spring fill the valleys and hills.
The mountain woodman cuts an armful of them
And brings them down to sell at the early market.
Things are cheap in proportion as they are common;
For two farthings, I buy a whole bundle.
I put the shoots in a great earthen pot
And heat them up along with boiling rice.
The purple nodules broken,—like an old brocade;
The white skin opened,—like new pearls.
Now every day I eat them recklessly;
For a long time I have not touched meat.
All the time I was living at Lo-yang
They could not give me enough to suit my taste,
Now I can have as many shoots as I please;
For each breath of the south-wind makes a new bamboo!

Having Climbed to the Topmost Peak
of the Incense-Burner Mountain

Up and up, the Incense-Burner Peak!
In my heart is stored what my eyes and ears perceived.
All the year—detained by official business;
To-day at last I got a chance to go.
Grasping the creepers, I clung to dangerous rocks;
My hands and feet—weary with groping for hold.
There came with me three or four friends,
But two friends dared not go further.
At last we reached the topmost crest of the Peak;
My eyes were blinded, my soul rocked and reeled.
The chasm beneath me—ten thousand feet;
The ground I stood on, only a foot wide.
If you have not exhausted the scope of seeing and hearing,
How can you realize the wideness of the world?
The waters of the River looked narrow as a ribbon,
P'ēn Castle smaller than a man's fist.
How it clings, the dust of the world's halter!
It chokes my limbs: I cannot shake it away.
Thinking of retirement,[1] I heaved an envious sigh,
Then, with lowered head, came back to the Ants' Nest.

[1] I.e., retirement from office.

211

Alarm at First Entering the
Yang-Tze Gorges

*(Written in A.D. 818, when he was being towed
up the rapids to Chung-chou.)*

Above, a mountain ten thousand feet high:
Below, a river a thousand fathoms deep.
A strip of green, walled by cliffs of stone:
Wide enough for the passage of a single reed.[1]
At Chü-t'ang a straight cleft yawns:
At Yen-yü islands block the stream.
Long before night the walls are black with dusk;
Without wind white waves rise.
The big rocks are like a flat sword:
The little rocks resemble ivory tusks.

[1] See Odes, v. 7.

We are stuck fast and cannot move a step.
How much the less, three hundred miles?[1]
Frail and slender, the twisted-bamboo rope:
Weak, the dangerous hold of the towers' feet.
A single slip—the whole convoy lost:
And *my* life hangs on *this* thread!
I have heard a saying "He that has an upright heart
Shall walk scathless through the lands of Man and Mo".[2]
How can I believe that since the world began
In every shipwreck none have drowned but rogues?
And how can I, born in evil days[3]
And fresh from failure,[4] ask a kindness of Fate?
Often I fear that these un-talented limbs
Will be laid at last in an un-named grave!

[1] The distance to Chung-chou.   [2] Dangerous savages.
[3] Of civil war.   [4] Alluding to his renewed banishment.

After Lunch

After lunch—one short nap:
On waking up—two cups of tea.
Raising my head, I see the sun's light
Once again slanting to the south-west.
Those who are happy regret the shortness of the day;
Those who are sad tire of the year's sloth.
But those whose hearts are devoid of joy or sadness
Just go on living, regardless of "short" or "long".

214

On Being Removed from Hsün-yang
and Sent to Chung-chou

A remote place in the mountains of Pa (Ssech'uan)

Before this, when I was stationed at Hsün-yang,
Already I regretted the fewness of friends and guests.
Suddenly, suddenly,—bearing a stricken heart
I left the gates, with nothing to comfort me.
Henceforward,—relegated to deep seclusion
In a bottomless gorge, flanked by precipitous mountains,
Five months on end the passage of boats is stopped
By the piled billows that toss and leap like colts.
The inhabitants of Pa resemble wild apes;
Fierce and lusty, they fill the mountains and prairies.
Among such as these I cannot hope for friends
And am pleased with anyone who is even remotely human!

Planting Flowers on the Embankment

(Written when Governor of Chung-chou)

I took money and bought flowering trees
And planted them out on the bank to the east of the Keep.
I simply bought whatever had most blooms,
Not caring whether peach, apricot, or plum.
A hundred fruits, all mixed up together;
A thousand branches, flowering in due rotation.
Each has its season coming early or late;
But to all alike the fertile soil is kind.
The red flowers hang like a heavy mist;
The white flowers gleam like a fall of snow.
The wandering bees cannot bear to leave them;
The sweet birds also come there to roost.
In front there flows an ever-running stream;
Beneath there is built a little flat terrace.
Sometimes I sweep the flagstones of the terrace;
Sometimes, in the wind, I raise my cup and drink.
The flower-branches screen my head from the sun;
The flower-buds fall down into my lap.
Alone drinking, alone singing my songs
I do not notice that the moon is level with the steps.
The people of Pa do not care for flowers;
All the spring no one has come to look.
But their Governor General, alone with his cup of wine
Sits till evening and will not move from the place!

216

Prose Letter to Yüan Chēn

(A. D. 818)

NIGHT of the tenth day of the fourth month. Lo-t'ien[1] says:
O Wei-chih,[2] Wei-chih, it is three years since I saw your face
and almost two years since I had a letter from you. Is man's
life so long that he can afford such partings? Much less should
hearts joined by glue be set in bodies remote as Hu and
Yüeh.[3] In promotion we could not be together; and in failure
we cannot forget each other. Snatched and wrenched apart,
separately each of us grows grey. O Wei-chih, what is to be
done? But this is the work of Heaven and there is no use in
speaking of it.

When I first arrived at Hsün-yang, Hsiung Ju-tēng[4] came
with the letter which you had written the year before, when
you were so ill. First you told me of the progress of your illness, next of your feelings while you were ill and last you
spoke of all our meetings and partings, and of the occasion of
your own difficulties and dangers. You had no time to write
more, but sent a bundle of your writings with a note attached,
which said, "Later on I will send a message by Po Minchung.[5]
Ask him for news and that will do instead of a letter". Alas!

---

[1] Other name of Po Chü-i.   [2] Other name of Yüan Chēn.
[3] The extreme North and South of China.
[4] A poet, several of whose short poems are well-known.
[5] The son of Po Chü-i's uncle Po Chi'-k'ang.

Is it thus that Wei-chih treats me? But again, I read the poem you wrote when you heard I had been banished:

The lamp had almost spent its light: shadows filled the room,
The night I heard that Lo-t'ien was banished to Kiu-kiang.
And I that had lain sick to death sat up suddenly in bed;
A dark wind blowing rain entered at the cold window.

If even strangers' hearts are touched by these lines, much more must mine be; so that to this day I cannot recite them without pain. Of this matter I will say no more, but tell you briefly what has passed of late.

It is more than three years since I came to Kiu-kiang. All this time my body has been strong and my heart much at peace. There has been no sickness in my household, even among the servants. Last summer my elder brother arrived from Hsü-chou, leading by the hand six or seven little brothers and sisters, orphans of various households. So that I have under my eyes all those who at present demand my care. They share with me cold and heat, hunger and satiety. This is my first consolation.

The climate of the River Province is somewhat cool, so that fevers and epidemics are rare. And while snakes and mosquitoes are few, the fish in the Pēn are remarkably fat, the River wine is exceedingly good, and indeed for the most part the food is like that of the North Country. Although the mouths within my doors are many and the salary of a Sub-Prefect is small, by a thrifty application of my means, I am yet able to provide for my household without seeking any

218

man's assistance to clothe their backs or fill their bellies. This is my second consolation.

In the autumn of last year I visited Lu Shan[1] for the first time. Reaching a point between the Eastern Forest and Western Forest Temples, beneath the Incense-Burner Peak, I was enamoured by the unequalled prospect of cloud-girt waters and spray-clad rocks. Unable to leave this place, I built a cottage here. Before it stand ten tall pines and a thousand tapering bamboos. With green creepers I fenced my garden; with white stones I made bridge and path. Flowing waters encircle my home; flying spray falls between the eaves. Red pomegranate and white lotus cluster on the steps of the pond. All is after this pattern, though I cannot here name each delight. Whenever I come here alone, I am moved to prolong my stay to ten days; for of the things that have all my life most pleased me, not one is missing. So that not only do I forget to go back, but would gladly end my days here. This is my third consolation.

Remembering that not having had news of me for so long, you might be in some anxiety with regard to me, I have hastened to set your mind at rest by recording these three consolations. What else I have to tell shall be set out in due order, as follows. . . .[2]

Wei-chih, Wei-chih! The night I wrote this letter I was sitting at the mountain-window of my thatched hut. I let my brush run as my hand willed and wrote at hazard as my

[1] A famous mountain near Kiu-kiang.
[2] What followed is omitted in the printed text.

thoughts came. When I folded it and addressed it, I found that dawn had come. I raised my head and saw only a few mountain-priests, some sitting, some sleeping. I heard the mournful cries of mountain apes and the sad twitterings of valley birds. O friend of all my life, parted from me by a thousand leagues, at such times as this "dim thoughts of the World"[1] creep upon me for a while; so, following my ancient custom, I send you these three couplets:

I remember how once I wrote you a letter sitting in the Palace at night,
At the back of the Hall of Golden Bells, when dawn was coming
        in the sky.
This night I fold your letter—in what place?
Sitting in a cottage on Lu Shan, by the light of a late lamp.
The caged bird and fettered ape are neither of them dead yet;
In the world of men face to face will they ever meet again?

O Wei-chih, Wei-chih! This night, this heart—do you know them or not? Lo-t'ien bows his head.

[1] This expression is used by Yüan Chēn in a poem addressed to Po Chü-i. By "the World", he means their life together at Court.

220

The Fifteenth Volume

Having completed the fifteenth volume of his works, the poet sends it to his friends Yüan Chēn and Li Chien, with a jesting poem.

(*Written in A. D. 818*)

My long poem, the "Eternal Grief",[1] is a beautiful and
    moving work;
My ten "Songs of Shensi" are models of tunefulness.
I cannot prevent Old Yüan from stealing my best rhymes;
But I earnestly beg Little Li to respect my ballads and songs.
While I am alive riches and honour will never fall to my lot;
But well I know that after I am dead the fame of my books
    will live.
This random talk and foolish boasting forgive me, for to-day
I have added Volume Fifteen to the row that stands
    to my name.

[1] See Giles, "Chinese Literature," p. 169.

Invitation to Hsiao Chü-shih[1]

(Written when Governor of Chung-chou)

Within the Gorges there is no lack of men;
They are people one meets, not people one cares for.
At my front door guests also arrive;
They are people one sits with, not people one knows.
When I look up, there are only clouds and trees;
When I look down—only my wife and child.
I sleep, eat, get up or sit still;
Apart from that, nothing happens at all.
But beyond the city Hsiao the hermit dwells;
And with *him* at least I find myself at ease.
For *he* can drink a full flagon of wine
And is good at reciting long-line poems.
Some afternoon, when the clerks have all gone home,
At a season when the path by the river bank is dry,
I beg you, take up your staff of bamboo-wood
And find your way to the parlour of the Government House.

---

[1] This poem, and those appearing on pp. 223, 224, and 225, were written
when the poet was Governor of a remote part of Szechuan, in the extreme
west of China.

To Li Chien

(A. D. 818)

The province I govern is humble and remote;
Yet our festivals follow the Courtly Calendar.
At rise of day we sacrificed to the Wind God,
When darkly, darkly, dawn glimmered in the sky.
Officers followed, horsemen led the way;
They brought us out to the wastes beyond the town,
Where river mists fall heavier than rain,
And the fires on the hill leap higher than the stars.

Suddenly I remembered the early levées at Court
When you and I galloped to the Purple Yard.
As we walked our horses up Dragon Tail Street
We turned our heads and gazed at the Southern Hills.
Since we parted, both of us have been growing old;
And our minds have been vexed by many anxious cares.
Yet even now I fancy my ears are full
Of the sound of jade tinkling on your bridle-straps.

The Spring River

(A. D. 820)

Heat and cold, dusk and dawn have crowded one upon
  the other;
Suddenly I find it is two years since I came to Chung-chou.
Through my closed doors I hear nothing but the morning
  and evening drum;
From my upper windows all I see is the ships that come
  and go.[1]
In vain the orioles tempt me with their song to stray beneath
  the flowering trees;
In vain the grasses lure me by their colour to sit beside
  the pond.
There is one thing and one alone I never tire of watching—
The spring river as it trickles over the stones and babbles
  past the rocks.

---

[1] "The Emperor Saga of Japan [reigned A. D. 810-23] one day quoted to
his Minister, Ono no Takamura, the couplet:
'Through my closed doors I hear nothing but the morning and evening drum;
From my upper windows in the distance I see ships that come and go.'

Takamura, thinking these were the Emperor's own verses, said: 'If I may
venture to criticize an august composition, I would suggest that the
phrase "in the distance" be altered.' The Emperor was delighted, for he
had purposely changed 'all I see' to 'in the distance I see'. At that time
there was only one copy of Po Chü-i's poems in Japan and the Emperor,
to whom it belonged, had allowed no one to see it."—From the *Kōdanshō*
[twelfth century].

224

After Collecting the Autumn Taxes

From my high castle I look at the town below
Where the natives of Pa cluster like a swarm of flies.
How can I govern these people and lead them aright?
I cannot even understand what they say.
But at least I am glad, now that the taxes are in,
To learn that in my province there is no discontent.
I fear its prosperity is not due to me
And was only caused by the year's abundant crops,
The papers that lie on my desk are simple and few;
My house by the moat is leisurely and still.
In the autumn rain the berries fall from the eaves;
At the evening bell the birds return to the wood.
A broken sunlight quavers over the southern porch
Where I lie on my couch abandoned to idleness.

225

Lodging with the Old Man
of the Stream

(A. D. 820)

Men's hearts love gold and jade;
Men's mouths covet wine and flesh.
Not so the old man of the stream;
He drinks from his gourd and asks nothing more.
South of the stream he cuts firewood and grass;
North of the stream he has built wall and roof.
Yearly he sows a single acre of land;
In spring he drives two yellow calves.
In these things he finds great repose;
Beyond these he has no wish or care.
By chance I met him walking by the water-side;
He took me home and lodged me in his thatched hut.
When I parted from him, to seek market and Court,
This old man asked my rank and pay.
Doubting my tale, he laughed loud and long:
"Privy Councillors do not sleep in barns".

To His Brother Hsing-chien

(A. D. 820)

Can the single cup of wine
We drank this morning have made my heart so glad?
This is a joy that comes only from within,
Which those who witness will never understand.
          I have but two brothers
And bitterly grieved that both were far away;
This Spring, back through the Gorges of Pa,
I have come to them safely, ten thousand leagues.
          Two sisters I had
Who had put up their hair, but not twined the sash;[1]
Yesterday both were married and taken away
By good husbands in whom I may well trust.
I am freed at last from the thoughts that made me grieve,
As though a sword had cut a rope from my neck.
And limbs grow light when the heart sheds its care:
Suddenly I seem to be flying up to the sky!

Hsing-chien, drink your cup of wine
Then set it down and listen to what I say.
Do not sigh that your home is far away;
Do not mind if your salary is small.
Only pray that as long as life lasts,
You and I may never be forced to part.

[1] I.e., got married.

The Pine-Trees in the Courtyard

(A.D. 820)

Below the hall
The pine-trees grow in front of the steps,
Irregularly scattered,—not in ordered lines.
Some are tall and some are low:
The tallest of them is six roods high;
The lowest but ten feet.
They are like wild things
And no one knows who planted them.
They touch the walls of my blue-tiled house;
Their roots are sunk in the terrace of white sand.
Morning and evening they are visited by the wind and moon;
Rain or fine,—they are free from dust and mud.
In the gales of autumn they whisper a vague tune;
From the suns of summer they yield a cool shade.
At the height of spring the fine evening rain
Fills their leaves with a load of hanging pearls.
At the year's end the time of great snow
Stamps their branches with a fret of glittering jade.
Of the Four Seasons each has its own mood;
Among all the trees none is like another.
Last year, when they heard I had bought this house,
Neighbours mocked and the World called me mad—
That a whole family of twice ten souls

228

Should move house for the sake of a few pines!
Now that I have come to them, what have they given me?
They have only loosened the buckles of my care.
Yet even so, they are "profitable friends",[1]
And fill my need of "converse with wise men".
Yet when I consider how, still a man of the world,
In belt and cap I scurry through dirt and dust,
From time to time my heart twinges with shame
That I am not fit to be master of my pines!

[1] See "Analects of Confucius" 4 and 5, where three kinds of "profitable friends" and three kinds of "profitable pleasures" are described; the third of the latter being "plenty of intelligent companions".

Sleeping on Horseback

(A. D. 822)

We had rode long and were still far from the inn;
My eyes grew dim; for a moment I fell asleep.
Under my right arm the whip still dangled;
In my left hand the reins for an instant slackened.
Suddenly I woke and turned to question my groom:
"We have gone a hundred paces since you fell asleep,"
Body and spirit for a while had exchanged place;
Swift and slow had turned to their contraries.
For these few steps that my horse had carried me
Had taken in my dream countless aeons of time!
True indeed is that saying of Wise Men
"A hundred years are but a moment of sleep".

Parting from the Winter Stove

(A. D. 822)

On the fifth day after the rise of Spring,
Everywhere the season's gracious altitudes!
The white sun gradually lengthening its course,
The blue-grey clouds hanging as though they would fall;
The last icicle breaking into splinters of jade;
The new stems marshalling red sprouts.
The things I meet are all full of gladness;
It is not only *I* who love the Spring.
To welcome the flowers I stand in the back garden;
To enjoy the sunlight I sit under the front eaves.
Yet still in my heart there lingers one regret;
Soon I shall part with the flame of my red stove!

Children

(Written circa A. D. 820)

My niece, who is six years old, is called "Miss Tortoise";
My daughter of three,—little "Summer Dress".
One is beginning to learn to joke and talk;
The other can already recite poems and songs.
At morning they play clinging about my feet;
At night they sleep pillowed against my dress.
Why, children, did you reach the world so late,
Coming to me just when my years are spent?
Young things draw our feelings to them;
Old people easily give their hearts.
The sweetest vintage at last turns sour;
The full moon in the end begins to wane.
And so with men the bonds of love and affection
Soon may change to a load of sorrow and care.
But all the world is bound by love's ties;
Why did I think that I alone should escape?

232

Pruning Trees

Trees growing,—right in front of my window;
The trees are high and the leaves grow thick.
Sad alas! the distant mountain view
Obscured by this, dimly shows between.
One morning I took knife and axe;
With my own hand I lopped the branches off.
Ten thousand leaves fall about my head;
A thousand hills come before my eyes.
Suddenly, as when clouds or mists break
And straight through, the blue sky appears;
Again, like the face of a friend one has loved
Seen at last after an age of parting.
First there came a gentle wind blowing;
One by one the birds flew back to the tree.
To ease my mind I gazed to the South East;
As my eyes wandered, my thoughts went far away.
Of men there is none that has not some preference;
Of things there is none but mixes good with ill.
It was not that I did not love the tender branches;
But better still,—to see the green hills!

Being Visited by a Friend
During Illness

I have been ill so long that I do not count the days;
At the southern window, evening—and again evening.
Sadly chirping in the grasses under my eaves
The winter sparrows morning and evening sing.
By an effort I rise and lean heavily on my bed;
Tottering I step towards the door of the courtyard.
By chance I meet a friend who is coming to see me;
Just as if I had gone specially to meet him.
They took my couch and placed it in the setting sun;
They spread my rug and I leaned on the balcony-pillar.
Tranquil talk was better than any medicine;
Gradually the feelings came back to my numbed heart.

On the Way to Hang-chow:
Anchored on the River at Night

Little sleeping and much grieving,—the traveller
Rises at midnight and looks back towards home.
The sands are bright with moonlight that joins the shores;
The sail is white with dew that has covered the boat.
Nearing the sea, the river grows broader and broader:
Approaching autumn, the nights longer and longer.
Thirty times we have slept amid mists and waves,
And still we have not reached Hang-chow!

Stopping the Night at Jung-yang

I grew up at Jung-yang;
I was still young when I left.
On and on,—forty years passed
Till again I stayed for the night at Jung-yang.
When I went away, I was only eleven or twelve;
This year I am turned fifty-six.
Yet thinking back to the times of my childish games,
Whole and undimmed, still they rise before me.
The old houses have all disappeared;
Down in the village none of my people are left.
It is not only that streets and buildings have changed;
But steep is level and level changed to steep!
Alone unchanged, the waters of Ch'iu and Yu
Passionless,—flow in their old course.

The Hat Given to the Poet
by Li Chien

Long ago a white-haired gentleman
You made the present of a black gauze hat.
The gauze hat still sits on my head;
But you already are gone to the Nether Springs.
The thing is old, but still fit to wear;
The man is gone and will never be seen again.
Out on the hill the moon is shining to-night
And the trees on your tomb are swayed by the
    autumn wind.

The Silver Spoon

While on the road to his new province, Hang-chow, in A.D. 822, he sends a silver spoon to his niece A-kuei, whom he had been obliged to leave behind with her nurse, old Mrs. Ts'ao.

To distant service my heart is well accustomed;
When I left home, it wasn't *that* which was difficult
But because I had to leave Miss Kuei at home—
For this it was that tears filled my eyes.
Little girls ought to be daintily fed:
Mrs. Ts'ao, please see to this!
That's why I've packed and sent a silver spoon;
You will think of me and eat up your food nicely!

The Big Rug

That so many of the poor should suffer from cold what can
      we do to prevent?
To bring warmth to a single body is not much use.
I wish I had a big rug ten thousand feet long,
Which at one time could cover up every inch of the City.

Good-bye to the People of Hang-chow

(A. D. 824)

Elders and officers line the returning road;
Wine and soup load the parting table.
I have not ruled you with the wisdom of Shao Kung;[1]
What is the reason your tears should fall so fast?
My taxes were heavy, though many of the people were poor;
The farmers were hungry, for often their fields were dry.
All I did was to dam the water of the Lake[2]
And help a little in a year when things were bad.

[1] A legendary ruler who dispensed justice sitting under a wild pear-tree.
[2] Po Chü-i built the dam on the Western Lake which is still known as "Po's dam".

240

Getting Up Early
on a Spring Morning

(Part of a poem written when Governor of Soochow in A.D. 825)

The early light of the rising sun shines on the beams
   of my house;
The first banging of opened doors echoes like the roll
   of a drum.
The dog lies curled on the stone step, for the earth is wet
   with dew;
The birds come near to the window and chatter, telling
   that the day is fine.
With the lingering fumes of yesterday's wine my head is
   still heavy;
With new doffing of winter clothes my body has
   grown light.

Written when Governor of Soochow

(A. D. 825)

A Government building, not my own home.
A Government garden, not my own trees.
But at Lo-yang I have a small house
And on Wei River I have built a thatched hut.
I am free from the ties of marrying and giving in marriage;
If I choose to retire, I have somewhere to end my days.
And though I have lingered long beyond my time,
To retire now would be better than not at all!

Losing A Slave-Girl

(Date uncertain)

Around my garden the little wall is low;
In the bailiff's lodge the lists are seldom checked.
I am ashamed to think we were not always kind;
I regret your labours, that will never be repaid.
The caged bird owes no allegiance;
The wind-tossed flower does not cling to the tree.

Where to-night she lies none can give us news;
Nor any knows, save the bright watching moon.

Lazy Man's Song

(A. D. 811)

I have got patronage, but am too lazy to use it;
I have got land, but am too lazy to farm it.
My house leaks; I am too lazy to mend it.
My clothes are torn; I am too lazy to darn them.
I have got wine, but am too lazy to drink;
So it's just the same as if my cellar were empty.
I have got a harp, but am too lazy to play;
So it's just the same as if it had no strings.
My wife tells me there is no more bread in the house;
I want to bake, but am too lazy to grind.
My friends and relatives write me long letters;
I should like to read them, but they're such a bother
    to open.
I have always been told that Chi Shu-yeh[1]
Passed his whole life in absolute idleness.
But he played the harp and sometimes transmuted metals,
So even *he* was not so lazy as I.

[1] Also known as Chi K'ang, a famous Quietist.

Baldridge

After Getting Drunk
Becoming Sober in the Night

Our party scattered at yellow dusk and I came home to bed;
I woke at midnight and went for a walk, leaning heavily
    on a friend.
As I lay on my pillow my vinous complexion, soothed by
    sleep, grew sober;
In front of the tower the ocean moon, accompanying the
    tide, had risen.
The swallows, about to return to the beams, went back to
    roost again;
The candle at my window, just going out, suddenly revived
    its light.
All the time till dawn came, still my thoughts were muddled;
And in my ears something sounded like the music of flutes
    and strings.

The Grand Houses at Lo-yang

(Circa A. D. 829)

By woods and water, whose houses are these
With high gates and wide-stretching lands?
From their blue gables gilded fishes hang;
By their red pillars carven coursers run.
Their spring arbours, warm with caged mist;
Their autumn yards with locked moonlight cold.
To the stem of the pine-tree amber beads cling;
The bamboo-branches ooze ruby-drops.
Of lake and terrace who may the masters be?
Staff-officers, Councillors-of-State.
All their lives they have never come to see,
But know their houses only from the bailiff's map!

246

The Cranes

(A. D. 830)

The western wind has blown but a few days;
Yet the first leaf already flies from the bough.
On the drying paths I walk in my thin shoes;
In the first cold I have donned my quilted coat.
Through shallow ditches the floods are clearing away;
Through sparse bamboos trickles a slanting light.
In the early dusk, down an alley of green moss,
The garden-boy is leading the cranes home.

On A Box
Containing His Own Works

I break up cypress and make a book-box;
The box well-made,—and the cypress-wood tough.
In it shall be kept what author's works?
The inscription says PO LO-T'IEN.
All my life has been spent in writing books,
From when I was young till now that I am old.
First and last,—seventy whole volumes;
Big and little,—three thousand themes.[1]
Well I know in the end they'll be scattered and lost;
But I cannot bear to see them thrown away,
With my own hand I open and shut the locks,
And put it carefully in front of the book-curtain.
I am like Tēng Pai-tao;[2]
But to-day there is not any Wang Ts'an.[3]
All I can do is to divide them among my daughters
To be left by them to give to my grandchildren.

[1] I.e., separate poems, essays, etc.
[2] Who was obliged to abandon his only child on the roadside.
[3] Who rescued a foundling.

On Being Sixty

Addressed to Liu Mēng-tē, who had asked for a poem.
He was the same age as Po Chü-i.

Between thirty and forty, one is distracted by the Five Lusts;
Between seventy and eighty, one is a prey to
 a hundred diseases.
But from fifty to sixty one is free from all ills;
Calm and still—the heart enjoys rest.
I have put behind me Love and Greed; I have done with
 Profit and Fame;
I am still short of illness and decay and far from
 decrepit age.
Strength of limb I still possess to seek the rivers and hills;
Still my heart has spirit enough to listen to flutes and strings.
At leisure I open new wine and taste several cups;
Drunken I recall old poems and sing a whole volume.
Mēng-tē has asked for a poem and herewith I exhort him
Not to complain of three-score, "the time of obedient ears".[1]

---

[1] Confucius said that it was not till *sixty* that "his ears obeyed him". This age was therefore called "the time of obedient ears".

On His Baldness

(A. D. 832)

At dawn I sighed to see my hairs fall;
At dusk I sighed to see my hairs fall.
For I dreaded the time when the last lock should go . . .
They are all gone and I do not mind at all!
I have done with that cumbrous washing and getting dry;
My tiresome comb for ever is laid aside.
Best of all, when the weather is hot and wet,
To have no top-knot weighing down on one's head!
I put aside my dusty conical cap;
          And loose my collar-fringe.
In a silver jar I have stored a cold stream;
On my bald pate I trickle a ladle-full.
Like one baptized with the Water of Buddha's Law,
I sit and receive this cool, cleansing joy.
Now I know why the priest who seeks Repose
Frees his heart by first shaving his head.

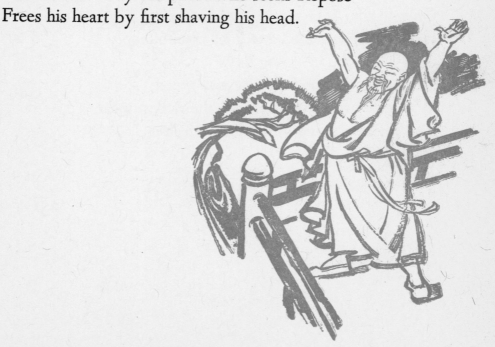

Thinking of the Past

(A. D. 833)

In an idle hour I thought of former days;
And former friends seemed to be standing in the room.
And then I wondered "Where are they now?"
Like fallen leaves they have tumbled to the Nether Springs.
Han Yü[1] swallowed his sulphur pills,
Yet a single illness carried him straight to the grave.
Yüan Chēn smelted autumn stone[2]
But before he was old, his strength crumbled away.
Master Tu possessed the "Secret of Health":
All day long he fasted from meat and spice.
The Lord Ts'ui, trusting a strong drug,
Through the whole winter wore his summer coat.
Yet some by illness and some by sudden death . . .
All vanished ere their middle years were passed.

Only I, who have never dieted myself
Have thus protracted a tedious span of age,
      I who in young days
Yielded lightly to every lust and greed;
Whose palate craved only for the richest meat
And knew nothing of bismuth or calomel.

[1] The famous poet, d. A. D. 824.
[2] Carbamide crystals.

When hunger came, I gulped steaming food;
When thirst came, I drank from the frozen stream.
With verse I served the spirits of my Five Guts;[1]
With wine I watered the three Vital Spots.
Day by day joining the broken clod
I have lived till now almost sound and whole.
There is no gap in my two rows of teeth;
Limbs and body still serve me well.
Already I have opened the seventh book of years;
Yet I eat my fill and sleep quietly;
I drink, while I may, the wine that lies in my cup,
And all else commit to Heaven's care.

[1] Heart, liver, stomach, lungs and kidney.

Old Age

Addressed to Liu Yü-hsi, who was born in the same year

(A. D. 835)

We are growing old together, you and I,
Let us ask ourselves, what is age like?
The dull eye is closed ere night comes;
The idle head, still uncombed at noon.
Propped on a staff, sometimes a walk abroad;
Or all day sitting with closed doors.
One dares not look in the mirror's polished face;
One cannot read small-letter books.
Deeper and deeper, one's love of old friends;
Fewer and fewer, one's dealings with young men.
One thing only, the pleasure of idle talk
Is great as ever, when you and I meet.

A Mad Poem Addressed to
My Nephews and Nieces

(A.D. 835)

The World cheats those who cannot read;
I, happily, have mastered script and pen.
The World cheats those who hold no office;
I am blessed with high official rank.
      The old are often ill;
I, at this day have not an ache or pain.
      They are often burdened with ties;
But I have finished with marriage and giving in marriage.
No changes happen to disturb the quiet of my mind;
No business comes to impair the vigour of my limbs.
Hence it is that now for ten years
Body and soul have rested in hermit peace.
And all the more, in the last lingering years
What I shall need are very few things.
A single rug to warm me through the winter;
One meal to last me the whole day.
It does not matter that my house is rather small;
One cannot sleep in more than one room!
It does not matter that I have not many horses;
One cannot ride in two coaches at once!
As fortunate as me among the people of the world

254

Possibly one would find seven out of ten.
As contented as me among a hundred men
Look as you may, you will not find one.
In the affairs of others even fools are wise;
In their own business even sages err.
To no one else would I dare to speak my heart,
So my wild words are addressed to my nephews and nieces.

To a Talkative Guest

(A. D. 836.)

The town visitor's easy talk flows in an endless stream;
The country host's quiet thoughts ramble timidly on.
"I beg you, Sir, do not tell me about things at Ch'ang-an;
For you entered just when my harp was tuned and lying
    balanced on my knees."

Climbing the Terrace of Kuan-yin and Looking at the City

Hundreds of houses, thousands of houses,—like a chessboard.
The twelve streets like a field planted with rows of cabbage.
In the distance perceptible, dim, dim—the fire of
    approaching dawn;

And a single row of stars lying to the west of the Five Gates.

Climbing the Ling Ying Terrace and Looking North

Mounting on high I begin to realize the smallness of
    Man's Domain;
Gazing into distance I begin to know the vanity of the
    Carnal World.
I turn my head and hurry home—back to the Court
    and Market,
A single grain of rice falling—into the Great Barn.

Dreaming of Yüan Chēn

(This was written eight years after Yüan Chēn's death,
when Po Chü-i was sixty-eight)

At night you came and took my hand and we wandered
   together in my dream;
When I woke in the morning there was no one to stop the
   tears that fell on my handkerchief.
On the banks of the Ch'ang my aged body three times[1] has
   passed through sickness;
At Hsien-yang[2] to the grasses on your grave eight times has
   autumn come.
You lie buried beneath the springs and your bones are
   mingled with the clay.
I—lodging in the world of men; my hair white as snow.
A-wei and Han-lang[3] both followed in their turn;
Among the shadows of the Terrace of Night did you know
   them or not?

[1] Since you died.
[2] Near Ch'ang-an, modern Si-ngan-fu.
[3] Affectionate names of Li Chien and Ts'ui Hsüan-liang.

Going to the Mountains
with a little Dancing Girl, Aged Fifteen

(Written when the poet was about sixty-five)

Two top-knots not yet plaited into one.
Of thirty years—just beyond half.
You who are really a lady of silks and satins
Are now become my hill and stream companion!
At the spring fountains together we splash and play:
On the lovely trees together we climb and sport.
Her cheeks grow rosy, as she quickens her sleeve-dancing:
Her brows grow sad, as she slows her song's tune.
Don't go singing the song of the Willow Branches,[1]
When there's no one here with a heart for you to break!

[1] A plaintive love-song, to which Po Chū-i had himself written words.

My Servant Wakes Me

(A.D. 839)

My servant wakes me: "Master, it is broad day.
Rise from bed; I bring you bowl and comb.
Winter comes and the morning air is chill;
To-day your Honour must not venture abroad."
When I stay at home, no one comes to call;
What must I do with the long, idle hours?
Setting my chair where a faint sunshine falls
I have warmed wine and opened my poetry-books.

Since I Lay Ill

(A. D. 840)

Since I lay ill, how long has passed?
Almost a hundred heavy-hanging days.
The maids have learnt to gather my medicine-herbs;
The dog no longer barks when the doctor comes.
The jars in my cellar are plastered deep with mould;
My singer's carpets are half crumbled to dust.
How can I bear, when the Earth renews her light,
To watch from a pillow the beauty of Spring unfold?

Song of Past Feelings

(Circa A. D. 840)

WHEN LO-T'IEN[1] was old, he fell ill of a palsy. So he made a list of his possessions and examined his expenses, that he might reject whatever had become superfluous. He had in his employ a girl about twenty years old called Fan Su, whose postures delighted him when she sang or danced. But above all she excelled in singing the "Willow Branch," so that many called her by the name of this song, and she was well known by this name in the town of Lo-yang. But she was on the list of unnecessary expenses and was to be sent away.

He had too a white horse with black mane, sturdy and sure-footed, which he had ridden for many years. It stood on the list of things which could be dispensed with, and was to be sold. When the groom led the horse through the gate, it tossed its head and looked back, neighing once with a sound in its voice that seemed to say: "I know I am leaving you and long to stay." Su, when she heard the horse neigh, rose timidly, bowed before me and spoke sweetly, as shall hereafter be shown. When she had done speaking her tears fell.

[1] I.e., Po Chü-i himself.

263

When first I heard Su's words, I was too sad to speak and could not answer her. But in a little while I ordered the bridle to be turned and the sleeve reversed. Then I gave her wine and drank a cup myself, and in my happiness sang a few score notes. And these notes turned into a poem, a poem without fixed measure, for the measure followed my irregular tune. In all there were 255 words.

Alas! I am no Sage. I could neither forget past feelings nor show such sensibility as this beast reputed incapable of feeling! Things that happen lay hold of my heart, and when my heart is moved, I cannot control it. Therefore, smiling at myself, I called this song "*A Song of Past Feelings Unforgotten.*"

The Song says:

> *I was selling my white horse*
> *And sending Willow Branch away.*
> *She covered her dark eyebrows;*
> *He trailed his golden halter.*
> *The horse, for want of speech,*
> *Neighed long and turned his head;*
> *And Willow Branch, twice bowing,*
> *Knelt long and spoke to me:*
> *"Master, you have ridden this horse five years,*
> *One thousand eight hundred days;*
> *Meekly he has borne the bit,*
> *Without shying, without bolting.*
> *And I have served you for ten years,*
> *Three thousand and six hundred days;*

Patient carrier of towel and comb,[1]
   Without complaint, without loss.
And now, though my shape is lowly,
   I am still fresh and strong.
And the colt is still in his prime,
   Without lameness or fault.
Why should you not use the colt's strength
   To replace your sick legs?
Why should you not use my song to gladden your
      casual cup?
Need you in one morning send both away,
   Send them away never to return?
This is what Su would say to you before she goes,
And this is what your horse meant also
   When he neighed at the gate.
Seeing my distress, who am a woman,
And hearing its cries, that is but a horse,
Shall our master alone remain pitiless?"

I looked up and sighed: I looked down and laughed.
Then I said:

     "Dear horse, stop your sad cries!
     Sweet Su, dry your bitter tears!
     For you shall go back to your stall;
     And you to the women's room.
     For though I am ill indeed,

[1] I.e., performing the functions of a wife.

And though my years are at their close,
The doom of Hsiang Chi[1] has not befallen me yet.
Must I in a single day
Lose the horse I rode and the lady I loved?
Su, O Su!
Sing once again the Song of the Willow Branch!
And I will pour you wine in that golden cup
And take you with me to the Land of Drunkenness."

[1] Who, surrounded at the battle of Kai-hsia (202 B. C.), gave his horse
to a boatman, lest it should fall into the hands of the enemy.

A Dream of Mountaineering

(Written when he was over seventy)

At night, in my dream, I stoutly climbed a mountain,
Going out alone with my staff of holly-wood.
A thousand crags, a hundred hundred valleys—
In my dream-journey none were unexplored
And all the while my feet never grew tired
And my step was as strong as in my young days.
Can it be that when the mind travels backward
The body also returns to its old state?
And can it be, as between body and soul,
That the body may languish, while the soul is still strong?
Soul and body—both are vanities:
Dreaming and waking—both alike unreal.
In the day my feet are palsied and tottering;
In the night my steps go striding over the hills.
As day and night are divided in equal parts—
Between the two, I *get* as much as I *lose*.

Ease

Congratulating himself on the comforts of his life
after his retirement from office. (Written circa A.D. 844)

Lined coat, warm cap and easy felt slippers,
In the little tower, at the low window, sitting over the
    sunken brazier.
Body at rest, heart at peace; no need to rise early.
I wonder if the courtiers at the Western Capital know of
    these things, or not?

The Philosophers

Lao-tzŭ

"Those who speak know nothing;
Those who know are silent."
These words, as I am told,
Were spoken by Lao-tzŭ.
If we are to believe that Lao-tzŭ
    Was himself *one who knew*,
How comes it that he wrote a book
    Of five thousand words?

Chuang-tzŭ, the Monist

Chuang-tzŭ levels all things
And reduces them to the same Monad.
But *I* say that even in their sameness
Difference may be found.
Although in following the promptings of
        their nature
They display the same tendency,
Yet it seems to me that in some ways
A phœnix is superior to a reptile!

On Hearing Someone Sing a Poem by Yüan Chēn

(Written long after Chēn's death)

No new poems his brush will trace:
    Even his fame is dead.
His old poems are deep in dust
    At the bottom of boxes and cupboards.
Once lately, when someone was singing,
    Suddenly I heard a verse—
Before I had time to catch the words
    A pain had stabbed my heart.

Illness

(*Written circa A.D. 842, when he was paralyzed*)

Dear friends, there is no cause for so much sympathy.
I shall certainly manage from time to time to take my
　　walks abroad.
All that matters is an active mind, what is the use of feet?
By land one can ride in a carrying-chair; by water, be rowed
　　in a boat.

Taoism and Buddhism

(Written shortly before his death)

A traveller came from across the seas
Telling of strange sights.
"In a deep fold of the sea-hills
I saw a terrace and tower.
In the midst there stood a Fairy Temple
With one niche empty.
They all told me this was waiting
For Lo-t'ien to come."

Traveller, I have studied the Empty Gate;[1]
I am no disciple of Fairies.
The story you have just told
Is nothing but an idle tale.
The hills of ocean shall never be
Lo-t'ien's home.
When I leave the earth it will be to go
To the Heaven of Bliss Fulfilled.[2]

---

[1] Buddhism. The poem is quite frivolous, as is shown by his claim to Bodhisattva-hood.
[2] The "tushita" Heaven, where Bodhisattvas wait till it is time for them to appear on earth as Buddhas.

Last Poem

They have put my bed beside the unpainted screen;
They have shifted my stove in front of the blue curtain.
I listen to my grandchildren, reading me a book;
I watch the servants, heating up my soup.
With rapid pencil I answer the poems of friends;
I feel in my pockets and pull out medicine-money.
When this superintendence of trifling affairs is done,
I lie back on my pillows and sleep with my face
     to the South.

[*Here End the Poems of Po Chü-i*]

The Little Lady of Ch'ing-hsi

[*A Children's Song*]

Her door opened on the white water
Close by the side of the timber bridge:
That's where the little lady lived
All alone without a lover.

what chance he had of winning the daughter, they answered: "The woman Li is possessed of considerable property, for her previous dealings have been with wealthy and aristocratic families, from whom she has received enormous sums. Unless you are willing to spend many thousand pounds, the daughter will have nothing to do with you."

The young man answered: "All I care about is to win her. I do not mind if she costs a million pounds." The next day he set out in his best clothes, with many servants riding behind him, and knocked at the door of Mrs. Li's house. Immediately a page-boy drew the bolt. The young man asked, "Can you tell me whose house this is?" The boy did not answer, but ran back into the house and called out at the top of his voice, "Here is the gentleman who dropped his whip the other day!"

Miss Li was evidently very much pleased. He heard her saying, "Be sure not to let him go away. I am just going to do my hair and change my clothes; I will be back in a minute". The young man, in high spirits, followed the page-boy into the house. A white-haired old lady was going upstairs, whom he took to be the girl's mother. Bowing low, the young man addressed her as follows: "I am told that you have a vacant plot of land, which you would be willing to let as building-ground. Is that true?" The old lady answered, "I am afraid the site is too mean and confined; it would be quite unsuitable for a gentleman's house. I should not like to offer it to you". She then took him into the guest-room, which was a very handsome one, and asked him to be seated, saying, "I have a daughter who has little either of beauty or accomplishment, but she is fond of seeing strangers. I should like you to meet her".

So saying, she called for her daughter, who presently entered. Her eyes sparkled with such fire, her arms were so dazzling white and there was in her movements such an exquisite grace that the young man could only leap to his feet in confusion and did not dare raise his eyes. When their salutations were over, he began to make a few remarks about the weather; and realized as he did so that her beauty was of a kind he had never encountered before.

They sat down again. Tea was made and wine poured out. The vessels used were spotlessly clean. He lingered till the day was almost over; the curfew-drum sounded its four beats. The old lady asked if he lived far away. He answered untruthfully, "Several leagues beyond the Yen-p'ing Gate", hoping that they would ask him to stay. The old lady said, "The drum has sounded. You will have to go back at once, unless you mean to break the law".

The young man answered, "I was being so agreeably entertained that I did not notice how rapidly the day had fled. My house is a long way off and in the city I have no friends or relations. What am I to do?" Miss Li then interposed, saying, "If you can forgive the meanness of our poor home, what harm would there be in your spending the night with us?" He looked doubtfully at the girl's mother, but met with no discouragement.

Calling his servants, he gave them money and told them to buy provisions for the night. But the girl laughingly stopped him, saying, "That is not the way guests are entertained. Our humble house will provide for your wants to-night, if you are willing to partake of our simple fare and defer your bounty to another occasion". He tried to refuse, but in the end she would not allow him to, and they all moved to the western hall. The curtains, screens, blinds and couches were of dazzling splendour; while the toilet-boxes, rugs, and pillows were of the utmost elegance. Candles were lighted and an excellent supper was served. After supper the old lady retired, leaving the lovers engaged in the liveliest conversation, laughing and chattering completely at their ease.

After a while the young man said: "I passed your house the other day and you happened to be standing at the door. And after that, I could think of nothing but you; whether I lay down to rest or sat down to eat, I could not stop thinking of you." She laughed and answered: "It was just the same with me." He said: "You must know that I did not come to-day simply to look for building-land. I came hoping that you would fulfil my lifelong desire; but I was not sure how you would welcome me. What—"

He had not finished speaking when the old woman came back and asked what they were saying. When they told her, she laughed and said, "Has not Mencius written that 'the relationship between men and women is the groundwork of society'? When lovers are agreed, not even the mandate of a parent will deter them. But my daughter is of humble birth. Are you sure that she is fit to 'present pillow and mat' to a great man?"

He came down from the daïs and, bowing low, begged that she would accept him as her slave. Henceforward the old lady regarded him as her son-in-law; they drank heavily together and finally parted. Next morning he had all his boxes and bags brought round to Mrs. Li's house and settled there permanently. Henceforward he shut himself up with his mistress and none of his friends ever heard of him. He consorted only with actors and dancers and low people of that kind, passing the time in wild sports and wanton feasting. When his money was all spent, he sold his horses and men-servants. In about a year his money, property, servants and horses were all gone.

For some time the old lady's manner towards him had been growing gradually colder, but his mistress remained as devoted as ever. One day she said to him, "We have been to-gether a year, but I am still not with child. They say that the spirit of the Bamboo Grove answers a woman's prayers as surely as an echo. Let us go to his temple and offer a libation".

The young man, not suspecting any plot, was delighted to take her to the temple, and having pawned his coat to buy sweet wine for the libation, he went with her and performed the ceremony of prayer. They stayed one night at the temple and came back next day. Whipping up their donkey, they soon arrived at the north gate of the P'ing-k'ang quarter. At this point his mistress turned to him and said, "My aunt's house is in a turning just near here. How would it be if we were to go there and rest for a little?"

He drove on as she directed him, and they had not gone more than a hundred paces, when he saw the entrance to a spacious carriage-drive. A servant who belonged to the place came out and stopped the cart, saying, "This is the entrance". The young man got down and was met by some one who came out and asked who they were. When told that it was Miss Li, he went back and announced her. Presently a mar-ried lady came out who seemed to be about forty. She greeted him, saying, "Has my niece arrived?" Miss Li then got out of the cart and her aunt said to her: "Why have you not been to see me for so long?" At which they looked at one another and laughed. Then Miss Li introduced him to her aunt and when that was over they all went into a side garden near the Western Halberd Gate. In the middle of the garden was a pagoda, and round it grew bamboos and trees of every variety, while ponds and summer-houses added to its air of seclusion. He asked Miss Li if this were her aunt's estate; she laughed, and spoke of something else.

Tea of excellent quality was served; but when they had been drinking it for a little while, a messenger came galloping up on a huge Fergana horse, saying that Miss Li's mother had suddenly been taken very ill and had already lost consciousness, so that they had better come back as quickly as possible.

Miss Li said to her aunt: "I am very much upset. I think I had better take the horse and ride on ahead. Then I will send it back, and you and my husband can come along later." The young man was anxious to go with her, but the aunt and her servants engaged him in conversation, flourishing their hands in front of him and preventing him from leaving the garden. The aunt said to him: "No doubt my sister is dead by this time. You and I ought to discuss together what can be done to help with the expenses of the burial. What is the use of running off like that? Stay here and help me to make a plan for the funeral and mourning ceremonies."

It grew late; but the messenger had not returned. The aunt said: "I am surprised he has not come back with the horse. You had better go there on foot as quickly as possible and see what has happened. I will come on later."

The young man set out on foot for Mrs. Li's house. When he got there he found the gate firmly bolted, locked and sealed. Astounded, he questioned the neighbours, who told him that the house had only been let to Mrs. Li and that, the lease having expired, the landlord had now resumed possession. The old lady, they said, had gone to live elsewhere. They did not know her new address.

At first he thought of hurrying back to Hsüan-yang and questioning the aunt; but he found it was too late for him to get there. So he pawned some of his clothes, and, with the proceeds, bought himself supper and hired a bed. But he was too angry and distressed to sleep, and did not once close his eyes from dusk till dawn. Early in the morning he dragged himself away and went to the "aunt's house". He knocked on the door repeatedly, but it was breakfast-time and no one answered. At last, when he had shouted several times at the top of his voice, a footman walked majestically to the door. The young man nervously mentioned the aunt's name and asked whether she was at home. The footman replied: "No one of that name here." "But she lived here yesterday evening", the young man protested; "why are you trying to deceive me? If she does not live here, who *does* the house belong to?" The footman answered: "This is the residence of His Excellency Mr. Ts'ui. I believe that yesterday some persons hired a corner of the grounds. I understand that they wished to entertain a cousin who was coming from a distance. But they were gone before nightfall."

The young man, perplexed and puzzled to the point of madness, was absolutely at a loss what to do next. The best he could think of was to go to the quarters in Pu-chēng, where he had installed himself when he first arrived at Ch'-ang-an. The landlord was sympathetic and offered to feed him. But the young man was too much upset to eat, and having fasted for three days fell seriously ill. He rapidly grew worse, and the landlord, fearing he would not recover, had him moved straight to the undertaker's shop. In a short time the whole of the undertaker's staff was collected round him, offering sympathy and bringing him food. Gradually he got better and was able to walk with a stick.

The undertaker now hired him by the day to hold up the curtains of fine cloth, by which he earned just enough to support himself. In a few months he grew quite strong again, but whenever he heard the mourners' doleful songs, in which they regretted that they could not change places with the corpse, burst into violent fits of sobbing and shed streams of tears over which they lost all control, then he used to go home and imitate their performance.

Being a man of intelligence, he very soon mastered the art and finally became the most expert mourner in Ch'-ang-an. It happened that there were two undertakers at this time between whom there was a great rivalry. The undertaker of the east turned out magnificent hearses and biers, and in this respect his superiority could not be contested. But the mourners he provided were somewhat inferior. Hearing of our young man's skill, he offered him a large sum for his services. The eastern undertaker's supporters, who were familiar with the repertoire of his company, secretly taught the young man several fresh tunes and showed him how to fit the words to them. The lessons went on for several weeks, without any one being allowed to know of it. At the end of that time the two undertakers agreed to hold a competitive exhibition of their wares in T'ien-mēn Street. The loser was to forfeit 50,000 cash to cover the cost of the refreshments provided. Before the exhibition an agreement was drawn up and duly signed by witnesses.

A crowd of several thousand people collected to watch the competition. The mayor of the quarter got wind of the proceedings and told the chief of police. The chief of police told the governor of the city. Very soon all the gentlemen of Ch'ang-an were hurrying to the spot and every house in the town was empty. The exhibition lasted from dawn till midday. Coaches, hearses and all kinds of funeral trappings were successively displayed, but the undertaker of the west could establish no superiority. Filled with shame, he set up a platform in the south corner of the square. Presently a man with a long beard came forward, carrying a hand-bell and attended by several assistants. He wagged his beard, raised his eyebrows, folded his arms across his chest and bowed. Then, mounting the platform, he sang the "Dirge of the White Horse". When it was over, confident of an easy victory, he glared round him, as if to imply that his opponents had all vanished. He was applauded on every side and was himself convinced that his talents were a unique product of the age and could not possibly be called into question.

After a while the undertaker of the east put together some benches in the north corner of the square, and a young man in a black hat came forward, attended by five assistants and carrying a bunch of hearse-plumes in his hand. It was the young man of our story.

He adjusted his clothes, looked timidly up and down, and then cleared his throat and began his tune with an air of great diffidence.

He sang the dirge "Dew on the Garlic".[1] His voice rose so shrill and clear that "its echoes shook the forest trees". Before he had finished the first verse, all who heard were sobbing and hiding their tears.

When the performance was over, every one made fun of the western undertaker, and he was so much put out that he immediately removed his exhibits and retired from the contest. The audience was amazed by the collapse of the western undertaker and could not imagine where his rival had procured so remarkable a singer.

[1] See page 33.

It happened that the Emperor had recently issued an order commanding the governors of outside provinces to confer with him at the capital at least once a year.

At this time the young man's father, who was governor of Ch'ang-chou, had recently arrived at the capital to make his report. Hearing of the competition, he and some of his colleagues discarded their official robes and insignia, and slipped away to join the crowd. With them was an old servant, who was the husband of the young man's foster-nurse. Recognizing his foster-son's way of moving and speaking, he was on the point of accosting him, but not daring to do so, he stood weeping silently. The father asked him why he was crying, and the servant replied, "Sir, the young man who is singing reminds me of your lost son". The father answered: "My son became the prey of robbers, because I gave him too much money. This cannot be he." So saying, he also began to weep and, leaving the crowd, returned to his lodging.

But the old servant went about among the members of the troupe, asking who it was that had just sung with such skill. They all told him it was the son of such a one; and when he asked the young man's own name, that too was unfamiliar, for he was living under an *alias*. The old servant was so much puzzled that he determined to put the matter to the test for himself. But when the young man saw his old friend walking towards him, he winced, turned away his face, and tried to hide in the crowd. The old man followed him and catching his sleeve, said: "Surely it is you!" Then they embraced and wept. Presently they went back together to his

287

father's lodging. But his father abused him, saying: "Your conduct has disgraced the family. How dare you show your face again?" So saying, he took him out of the house and led him to the ground between the Ch'ü-chiang Pond and the Apricot Gardens. Here he stripped him naked and thrashed him with a horse-whip, till the young man succumbed to the pain and collapsed. The father then left him and went away.

But the young man's singing-master had told some of his friends to watch what happened to him. When they saw him stretched inanimate on the ground, they came back and told the other members of the troupe.

The news occasioned universal lamentation, and two men were despatched with a reed mat to cover up the body. When they got there they found his heart still warm, and when they had held him in an upright posture for some time, his breathing recommenced. So they carried him home between them and administered liquid food through a reed-pipe. Next morning, he recovered consciousness; but after several months he was still unable to move his hands and feet. Moreover, the sores left by his thrashing festered in so disgusting a manner that his friends found him too troublesome, and one night deposited him in the middle of the road. However, the passers-by, harrowed by his condition, never failed to throw him scraps of food.

So copious was his diet that in three months he recovered sufficiently to hobble with a stick. Clad in a linen coat,— which was knotted together in a hundred places, so that it looked as tattered as a quail's tail,—and carrying a broken saucer in his hand, he now went about the idle quarters of the town, earning his living as a professional beggar.

Autumn had now turned to winter. He spent his nights in public lavatories and his days haunting the markets and booths.

One day when it was snowing hard, hunger and cold had driven him into the streets. His beggar's cry was full of woe and all who heard it were heart-rent. But the snow was so heavy that hardly a house had its outer door open, and the streets were empty.

When he reached the eastern gate of An-i, about the seventh or eighth turning north of the Hsün-li Wall, there was a house with the double-doors half open.

It was the house where Miss Li was then living, but the young man did not know.

He stood before the door, wailing loud and long.

Hunger and cold had given such a piteous accent to his cry that none could have listened unmoved.

Miss Li heard it from her room and at once said to her servant, "That is so-and-so. I know his voice". She flew to the door and was horrified to see her old lover standing before her so emaciated by hunger and disfigured by sores that he seemed scarcely human. "Can it be you?" she said. But the young man was so overcome by bewilderment and excitement that he could not speak, but only moved his lips noiselessly.

She threw her arms round his neck, then wrapped him in her own embroidered jacket and led him to the parlour. Here,

289

with quavering voice, she reproached herself, saying, "It is my doing that you have been brought to this pass". And with these words she swooned.

Her mother came running up in great excitement, asking who had arrived. Miss Li, recovering herself, said who it was. The old woman cried out in rage: "Send him away! What did you bring him in here for?"

But Miss Li looked up at her defiantly and said: "Not so! This is the son of a noble house. Once he rode in grand coaches and wore golden trappings on his coat. But when he came to our house, he soon lost all he had; and then we plotted together and left him destitute. Our conduct has indeed been inhuman! We have ruined his career and robbed

him even of his place in the category of human relationships. For the love of father and son is implanted by Heaven; yet we have hardened his father's heart, so that he beat him with a stick and left him on the ground.

"Every one in the land knows that it is I who have reduced him to his present plight. The Court is full of his kinsmen. Some day one of them will come into power. Then an inquiry will be set afoot, and disaster will overtake us. And since we have flouted Heaven and defied the laws of humanity, neither spirits nor divinities will be on our side. Let us not wantonly incur a further retribution!

"I have lived as your daughter for twenty years. Reckoning what I have cost you in that time, I find it must be close on a thousand pieces of gold. You are now aged sixty, so that by the price of twenty more years' food and clothing, I can buy my freedom. I intend to live separately with this young man. We will not go far away; I shall see to it that we are near enough to pay our respects to you both morning and evening."

The "mother" saw that she was not to be gainsaid and fell in with the arrangement. When she had paid her ransom, Miss Li had a hundred pieces of gold left over; and with them she hired a vacant room, five doors away. Here she gave the young man a bath, changed his clothes, fed him with hot soup to relax his stomach, and later on fattened him up with cheese and milk. In a few weeks she began to place before him all the choicest delicacies of land and sea; and she clothed him with cap, shoes and stockings of the finest quality. In a short time he began gradually to put on flesh, and by the end of the year, he had entirely recovered his former health.

One day Miss Li said to him: "Now your limbs are stout again and your will strong! Sometimes, when deeply pondering in silent sorrow, I wonder to myself how much you remember of your old literary studies?" He thought and answered: "Of ten parts I remember two or three."

Miss Li then ordered the carriage to be got ready and the young man followed her on horseback. When they reached the classical bookshop at the side-gate south of the Flag-tower, she made him choose all the books he wanted, till she had laid out a hundred pieces of gold. Then she packed them in the cart and drove home. She now made him dismiss all other thoughts from his mind and apply himself only to study. All the evening he toiled at his books, with Miss Li at his side, and they did not retire till midnight. If ever she found that he was too tired to work, she made him lay down his classics and write a poem or ode.

In two years he had thoroughly mastered his subjects and was admired by all the scholars of the realm. He said to Miss Li, "*Now*, surely, I am ready for the examiners!" but she would not let him compete and made him revise all he had learnt, to prepare for the "hundredth battle". At the end of the third year she said, "Now you may go". He went in for the examination and passed at the first attempt. His reputation spread rapidly through the examination rooms and even older men, when they saw his compositions, were filled with admiration and respect, and sought his friendship.

But Miss Li would not let him make friends with them, saying, "Wait a little longer! Nowadays when a bachelor of arts has passed his examination, he thinks himself fit to hold the most advantageous posts at Court and to win a universal reputation. But your unfortunate conduct and disreputable past put you at a disadvantage beside your fellow-scholars. You must 'grind, temper and sharpen' your attainments, that you may secure a second victory. Then you will be able to match yourself against famous scholars and contend with the illustrious".

The young man accordingly increased his efforts and enhanced his value. That year it happened that the Emperor had decreed a special examination for the selection of candidates of unusual merit from all parts of the Empire. The young man competed, and came out top in the "censorial essay". He was offered the post of Army Inspector at Ch'ēng-tu Fu. The officers who were to escort him were all previous friends.

When he was about to take up his post, Miss Li said to him, "Now that you are restored to your proper station in life, I will not be a burden to you. Let me go back and look after the old lady till she dies. You must ally yourself with some lady of noble lineage, who will be worthy to carry the sacrificial dishes in your Ancestral Hall. Do not injure your prospects by an unequal union. Good-bye, for now I must leave you".

The young man burst into tears and threatened to kill himself if she left him, but she obstinately refused to go with him. He begged her passionately not to desert him, and she at last consented to go with him across the river as far as Chien-mēn.[1] "There", she said, "you must part with me". The young man consented and in a few weeks they reached Chien-mēn. Before he had started out again, a proclamation arrived announcing that the young man's father, who had been Governor of Ch'ang-chou, had been appointed Governor of Ch'ēng-tu and Intendant of the Chien-nan Circuit. Next morning the father arrived, and the young man sent in his card and waited upon him at the posting-station. His father did not recognize him, but the card bore the names of the young man's father and grandfather, with their ranks and titles. When he read these, he was astounded, and bidding his son mount the steps he caressed him and wept. After a while he said: "Now we two are father and son once more," and bade him tell his story. When he heard of the young man's adventures, he was amazed. Presently he asked: "And where is Miss Li?" He replied: "She came with me as far as here, but now she is going back again."

"I cannot allow it", the father said. Next day he ordered a carriage for his son and sent him on to report himself at Ch'ēng-tu; but he detained Miss Li at Chien-mēn, found her a suitable lodging and ordered a match-maker to perform the initial ceremonies for uniting the two families and to accomplish the six rites of welcome. The young man came back from Ch'ēng-tu and they were duly married. In the years that followed their marriage, Miss Li showed herself a devoted

[1] The "Sword-gate": commanding the pass which leads into Szechuan from the north.

wife and competent housekeeper, and was beloved by all her relations.

Some years later both the young man's parents died, and in his mourning observances he showed unusual piety. As a mark of divine favour, magic toadstools grew on the roof of his mourning-hut,[1] each stem bearing three plants. The report of his virtue reached even the Emperor's ears. Moreover, a number of white swallows nested in the beams of his roof, an omen which so impressed the Emperor that he raised his rank immediately.

When the three years of mourning were over, he was successively promoted to various distinguished posts and in the

[1] See "Book of Rites", xxxii, 3. On returning from his father's burial a son must not enter the house; he should live in an "out-house", mourning for his father's absence.

course of ten years was Governor of several provinces. Miss Li was given the fief of Chien-kuo, with the title "The Lady of Chien-kuo".

He had four sons who all held high rank. Even the least successful of them became Governor of T'ai-yüan, and his brothers all married into great families, so that his good fortune both in public and private life was without parallel.

How strange that we should find in the conduct of a prostitute a degree of constancy rarely equalled even by the heroines of history! Surely the story is one which cannot but provoke a sigh!

My great-uncle was Governor of Chin-chou; subsequently he joined the Ministry of Finance and became Inspector of Waterways, and finally Inspector of Roads. In all these three offices he had Miss Li's husband as his colleague, so that her story was well known to him in every particular. During the Chēng-yüan period[1] I was sitting one day with Li Kung-tso[2] of Lung-hai; we fell to talking of wives who had distinguished themselves by remarkable conduct. I told him the story of Miss Li. He listened with rapt attention, and when it was over, asked me to write it down for him. So I took up my brush, wetted the hairs and made this rough outline of the story.

[Dated] *Autumn, eighth month of the year Yi-hai (A. D. 795)*

---

[1] A. D. 785-805.   [2] A writer.

The Pitcher

By *Yüan Chēn* (*A. D.* 779-831)

I dreamt I climbed to a high, high plain;
And on the plain I found a deep well.
My throat was dry with climbing and I longed to drink;
And my eyes were eager to look into the cool shaft.
I walked round it; I looked right down;
I saw my image mirrored on the face of the pool.
An earthen pitcher was sinking into the black depths;
There was no rope to pull it to the well-head.
I was strangely troubled lest the pitcher should be lost,
And started wildly running to look for help.
From village to village I scoured that high plain;
The men were gone: the dogs leapt at my throat.
I came back and walked weeping round the well;
Faster and faster the blinding tears flowed—
Till my own sobbing suddenly woke me up;
My room was silent; no one in the house stirred;
The flame of my candle flickered with a green smoke;
The tears I had shed glittered in the candle-light.
A bell sounded; I knew it was the midnight-chime;
I sat up in bed and tried to arrange my thoughts:

The plain in my dream was the graveyard at Ch'ang-an,
Those hundred acres of untilled land.
The soil heavy and the mounds heaped high;
And the dead below them laid in deep troughs.
Deep are the troughs, yet sometimes dead men
Find their way to the world above the grave.
And to-night my love who died long ago
Came into my dream as the pitcher sunk in the well.
That was why the tears suddenly streamed from my eyes,
Streamed from my eyes and fell on the collar of my dress.

The Story of Ts'ui Ying-ying

By Yüan Chēn (A. D. 799–831)

DURING the Chēng-yüan[1] period of the T'ang dynasty there lived a man called Chang.[2] His nature was gentle and refined, and his person of great beauty. But his deeper feelings were resolutely held in restraint, and he would indulge in no license. Sometimes his friends took him to a party and he would try to join their frolics; but when the rest were shouting and scuffling their hardest, Chang only pretended to take his share. For he could never overcome his shyness. So it came about that though already twenty-three, he had not yet enjoyed a woman's beauty. To those who questioned him he answered, "It is not such as Master Tēng-t'u[3] who are true lovers of beauty; for they are merely profligates. I consider myself a lover of beauty, who happens never to have met with it. And I am of this opinion because I know that, in other things, whatever is beautiful casts its spell upon me; so that I cannot be devoid of feeling". His questioners only laughed.

[1] A. D. 785-805.   [2] I.e., Yüan Chēn himself.
[3] Type of the indiscriminate lover, fourth century B. C.

299

About this time Chang went to Puchow. Some two miles east of the town there is a temple called the P'-u-chiu-ssŭ, and here he took up his lodging. Now it happened that at this time the widow of a certain Ts'ui was returning to Ch'ang-an.[1] She passed through Puchow on her way and stayed at the same temple. This lady was born of the Chēng family and Chang's mother was also a Chēng. He unravelled their relationship and found that they were second-cousins.

This year General Hun-Chan[2] died at Puchow. There was a certain Colonel Ting Wēn-ya who ill-treated his troops. The soldiers accordingly made Hun-Chan's funeral the occasion of a mutiny, and began to plunder the town. The Ts'ui family had brought with them much valuable property and many slaves. Subjected to this sudden danger when far from home, they had no one from whom they could seek protection.

Now it happened that Chang had been friendly with the political party to which the commander at Puchow belonged. At his request a guard was sent to the temple and no disorder took place there. A few days afterwards the Civil Commissioner Tu Chio was ordered by the Emperor to take over the command of the troops. The mutineers then laid down their arms.

The widow Chēng was very sensible of the service which Chang had rendered. She therefore provided dainties and invited him to a banquet in the middle hall. At table she

[1] The capital of China at that time; now called Hsi-an-fu.
[2] Born A. D. 735; died 799. Famous for his campaigns against the Tibetans and Uighurs.

300

turned to him and said, "I, your cousin, a lonely and widowed relict, had young ones in my care. If we had fallen into the hands of the soldiery, I could not have helped them. Therefore the lives of my little boy and young daughter were saved by your protection, and they owe you eternal gratitude. I will

now cause them to kneel before you, their merciful cousin, that they may thank you for your favours". First she sent for her son, Huan-lang, who was about ten years old, a handsome and gentle child. Then she called to her daughter, Ying-ying: "Come and bow to your cousin. Your cousin saved your life."

301

For a long while she would not come, saying that she was not well. The widow grew angry and cried: "Your cousin saved your life. But for his help, you would now be a prisoner. How can you treat him so rudely?"

At last she came in, dressed in everyday clothes, with a look of deep unhappiness in her face. She had not put on any ornaments. Her hair hung down in coils, the black of her two eyebrows joined, her cheeks were not rouged. But her features were of exquisite beauty and shone with an almost dazzling lustre.

Chang bowed to her, amazed. She sat down by her mother's side and looked all the time towards her, turning from him with a fixed stare of aversion, as though she could not endure his presence.

He asked how old she was. The widow answered, "She was born in the year of the present Emperor's reign that was a year of the Rat, and now it is the year of the Dragon in the period Chēng-yüan.[1] So she must be seventeen years old".

Chang tried to engage her in conversation, but she would not answer, and soon the dinner was over. He was passionately in love with her and wanted to tell her so, but could find no way.

Ying-ying had a maid-servant called Hung-niang, whom Chang sometimes met and greeted. Once he stopped her and was beginning to tell her of his love for her mistress; but she was frightened and ran away. Then Chang was sorry he had not kept silence.

[1] I.e., A. D. 800.

Next day he met Hung-niang again, but was ashamed and did not say what was in his mind. But this time the maid herself broached the subject and said to Chang, "Master, I dare not tell her what you told me, or even hint at it. But since your mother was a kinswoman of the Ts'uis, why do you not seek my mistress's hand on that plea?"

Chang said, "Since I was a child in arms, my nature has been averse to intimacy. Sometimes I have idled with wearers of silk and gauze, but my fancy was never once detained. I little thought that in the end I should be entrapped.

"Lately at the banquet I could scarcely contain myself; and since then, when I walk, I forget where I am going and when I eat, I forget to finish my meal, and do not know how to endure the hours from dawn to dusk.

"If we were to get married through a matchmaker and perform the ceremonies of Sending Presents and Asking Names, it would take many months, and by that time you would have to look for me 'in the dried-fish shop'. What is the use of giving me such advice as that?"

The maid replied, "My mistress clings steadfastly to her chastity, and even an equal could not trip her with lewd talk. Much less may she be won through the stratagems of a maid-servant. But she is skilled in composition, and often when she has made a poem or essay, she is restless and dissatisfied for a long while after. You must try to provoke her by a love-poem. There is no other way".

Chang was delighted and at once composed two Spring Poems to send her. Hung-niang took them away and came back the same evening with a coloured tablet, which she gave to Chang, saying, "This is from my mistress". It bore the title "The Bright Moon of the Fifteenth Night". The words ran:

To wait for the moon I am sitting in the western parlour;
To greet the wind, I have left the door ajar.
When a flower's shadow stirred and brushed the wall,
For a moment I thought it the shadow of a lover coming.

Chang could not doubt her meaning. That night was the fourth after the first decade of the second month. Beside the eastern wall of Ts'ui's apartments there grew an apricot-tree; by climbing it one could cross the wall. On the next night (which was the night of the full moon) Chang used the tree as a ladder and crossed the wall. He went straight to the western parlour and found the door ajar. Hung-niang lay asleep on the bed. He woke her, and she cried in a voice of astonishment, "Master Chang, what are you doing here?" Chang answered, half-truly: "Ts'ui's letter invited me. Tell her I have come." Hung-niang soon returned, whispering, "She is coming, she is coming". Chang was both delighted and surprised, thinking that his salvation was indeed at hand.

At last Ts'ui entered.

Her dress was sober and correct, and her face was stern. She at once began to reprimand Chang, saying, "I am grateful for the service which you rendered to my family. You gave support to my dear mother when she was at a loss how to save her little boy and young daughter. How came you to send me a wicked message by the hand of a low maid-servant? In protecting me from the license of others, you acted nobly. But now that you wish to make me a partner to your own licentious desires, you are asking me to accept one wrong in exchange for another.

"How was I to repel this advance? I would gladly have hidden your letter, but it would have been immoral to harbour a record of illicit proposals. Had I shown it to my mother, I should ill have requited the debt we owe you. Were I to entrust a message of refusal to a servant or concubine, I feared it might not be truly delivered. I thought of writing a letter to tell you what I felt; but I was afraid I might not be able to make you understand. So I sent those trivial verses, that I might be sure of your coming. I have no cause to be ashamed of an irregularity which had no other object but the preservation of my chastity".

With these words she vanished. Chang remained for a

long while petrified with astonishment. At last he climbed back over the wall and went home in despair.

Several nights after this he was lying asleep near the verandah, when some one suddenly woke him. He rose with a startled sigh and found that Hung-niang was there, with bed-clothes under her arm and a pillow in her hand. She shook Chang, saying, "She is coming, she is coming. Why are you asleep?" Then she arranged the bed-clothes and pillow and went away.

Chang sat up and rubbed his eyes. For a long while he thought he must be dreaming, but he assumed a respectful attitude and waited.

Suddenly Hung-niang came back, bringing her mistress with her. Ts'ui, this time, was languid and flushed, yielding and wanton in her air, as though her strength could scarcely support her limbs. Her former severity had utterly disappeared.

That night was the eighth of the second decade. The crystal beams of the sinking moon twinkled secretly across their bed. Chang, in a strange exaltation, half-believed that a fairy had come to him, and not a child of mortal men.

At last the temple bell sounded, dawn glimmered in the sky and Hung-niang came back to fetch her mistress away. Ts'ui turned on her side with a pretty cry, and followed her maid to the door.

The whole night she had not spoken a word.

Chang rose when it was half-dark, still thinking that perhaps it had been a dream. But when it grew light, he saw her

306

powder on his arm and smelt her perfume in his clothes. A tear she had shed still glittered on the mattress.

For more than ten days afterwards he did not see her again. During this time he began to make a poem called "Meeting a Fairy", in thirty couplets. It was not yet finished, when he chanced to meet Hung-niang in the road. He asked her to take the poem to Ts'ui.

After this Ts'ui let him come to her, and for a month or more he crept out at dawn and in at dusk, the two of them living together in that western parlour of which I spoke before.

Chang often asked her what her mother thought of him. Ts'ui said, "I know she would not oppose my will. So why should we not get married at once?"

Soon afterwards, Chang had to go to the capital. Before starting, he tenderly informed her of his departure. She did not reproach him, but her face showed pitiable distress. On the night before he started, he was not able to see her.

After spending a few months in the west, Chang returned to Puchow and again lodged for several months in the same building as the Ts'uis. He made many attempts to see Ying-ying alone, but she would not let him do so. Remembering that she was fond of calligraphy and verse, he frequently sent her his own compositions, but she scarcely glanced at them.

It was characteristic of her that when any situation was at its acutest point, she appeared quite unconscious of it. She talked glibly, but would seldom answer a question. She expected absolute devotion, but herself gave no encouragement.

Sometimes when she was in the depth of despair, she would affect all the while to be quite indifferent. It was rarely possible to know from her face whether she was pleased or sorry.

One night Chang came upon her unawares when she was playing on the harp, with a touch full of passion. But when she saw him coming, she stopped playing. This incident increased his infatuation.

Soon afterwards, it became time for him to compete in the Literary Examinations, and he was obliged once more to set out for the western capital.

The evening before his departure, he sat in deep despondency by Ts'ui's side, but did not try again to tell her of his love. Nor had he told her that he was going away, but she seemed to have guessed it, and with submissive face and gentle voice, she said to him softly: "Those whom a man leads astray, he will in the end abandon. It must be so, and I will not reproach you. You deigned to corrupt me and now you deign to leave me. That is all. And your vows of 'faithfulness till death'—they too are cancelled. There is no need for you to grieve at this parting, but since I see you so sad and can give you no other comfort—you once praised my harp-playing; but I was bashful and would not play to you. Now I am bolder, and if you choose, I will play you a tune."

She took her harp and began the prelude to "Rainbow Skirts and Feather Jackets".[1] But after a few bars the tune broke off into a wild and passionate dirge.

[1] A gay court tune of the eighth century.

All who were present caught their breath; but in a moment she stopped playing, threw down her harp and, weeping bitterly, ran to her mother's room.

She did not come back.

Next morning Chang left. The following year he failed in his examinations and could not leave the capital. So, to unburden his heart, he wrote a letter to Ts'ui. She answered him somewhat in this fashion: "I have read your letter and cherish it dearly. It has filled my heart half with sorrow, half with joy. You sent with it a box of garlands and five sticks of paste, that I may decorate my head and colour my lips.

"I thank you for your presents; but there is no one now to care how I look. Seeing these things only makes me think of you and grieve the more.

"You say that you are prospering in your career at the capital, and I am comforted by that news. But it makes me fear you will never come back again to one who is so distant and humble. But *that* is settled for ever, and it is no use talking of it.

"Since last autumn I have lived in a dazed stupor. Amid the clamour of the daytime, I have sometimes forced myself to laugh and talk; but alone at night I have done nothing but weep. Or, if I have fallen asleep my dreams have always been full of the sorrows of parting. Often I dreamt that you came to me as you used to do, but always before the moment of our joy your phantom vanished from my side. Yet, though we are still bedfellows in my dreams, when I wake and think of it, the time when we were together seems very far off. For since we parted, the old year has slipped away and a new year has begun. . . .

"Ch'ang-an is a city of pleasure, where there are many snares to catch a young man's heart. How can I hope that you will not forget one so sequestered and insignificant as I? And indeed, if you were to be faithful, so worthless a creature could never requite you. But our vows of unending love—those I at least can fulfil.

"Because you are my cousin, I met you at the feast. Lured by a maid-servant, I visited you in private. A girl's heart is not in her own keeping. You 'tempted me by your ballads'[1] and I could not bring myself to 'throw the shuttle'.[2]

"Then came the sharing of pillow and mat, the time of perfect loyalty and deepest tenderness. And I, being young and foolish, thought it would never end.

"Now, having 'seen my Prince',[3] I cannot love again; nor, branded by the shame of self-surrender, am I fit to perform 'the service of towel and comb';[4] and of the bitterness of the long celibacy which awaits me, what need is there to speak?

"The good man uses his heart; and if by chance his gaze has fallen on the humble and insignificant, till the day of his death, he continues the affections of his life. The cynic cares nothing for people's feelings. He will discard the small to follow the great, look upon a former mistress merely as an ac-

[1] As Ssŭ-ma tempted Cho Wēn-chün, second century B. C.
[2] As the neighbour's daughter did to Hsieh Kun (A. D. fourth century), in order to repel his advances.
[3] Odes I. 1., X. 2.   [4] = become a bride.

310

complice in sin, and hold that the most solemn vows are made only to be broken. He will reverse all natural laws—as though Nature should suddenly let bone dissolve, while cinnabar resisted the fire. The dew that the wind has shaken from the tree still looks for kindness from the dust; and such, too, is the sum of *my* hopes and fears.

"As I write, I am shaken by sobs and cannot tell you all that is in my heart. My darling, I am sending you a jade ring that I used to play with when I was a child. I want you to wear it at your girdle, that you may become firm and flawless as this jade, and, in your affections, unbroken as the circuit of this ring.

"And with it I am sending a skein of thread and a tea-trough of flecked bamboo. There is no value in these few things. I send them only to remind you to keep your heart pure as jade and your affection unending as this round ring. The bamboo is mottled as if with tears, and the thread is tangled as the thoughts of those who are in sorrow. By these tokens I seek no more than that, knowing the truth, you may think kindly of me for ever.

"Our hearts are very near, but our bodies are far apart. There is no time fixed for our meeting; yet a secret longing can unite souls that are separated by a thousand miles.

"Protect yourself against the cold spring wind, eat well—look after yourself in all ways and do not worry too much about your worthless handmaid,

Ts'ui Ying-ying."

311

Chang showed this letter to his friends and so the story became known to many who lived at that time. All who heard it were deeply moved; but Chang, to their disappointment, declared that he meant to break with Ts'ui. Yüan Chēn, of Honan, who knew Chang well, asked him why he had made this decision.

Chang answered:

"I have observed that in Nature whatever has perfect beauty is either itself liable to sudden transformations or else is the cause of them in others. If Ts'ui were to marry a rich gentleman and become his pet, she would for ever be changing, as the clouds change to rain, or as the scaly dragon turns into the horned dragon. I, for one, could never keep pace with her transformations.

"Of old, Hsin of the Yin dynasty and Yu of the Chou dynasty ruled over kingdoms of many thousand chariots, and their strength was very great. Yet a single woman brought them to ruin, dissipating their hosts and leading these monarchs to the assassin's knife. So that to this day they are a laughing-stock to all the world. I know that my constancy could not withstand such spells, and that is why I have curbed my passion."

At these words all who were present sighed deeply.

A few years afterwards Ts'ui married some one else and Chang also found a wife. Happening once to pass the house where Ts'ui was living, he called on her husband and asked to see her, saying he was her cousin. The husband sent for

312

her, but she would not come. Chang's vexation showed itself in his face. Some one told Ts'ui of this and she secretly wrote the poem:

> Since I have grown so lean, my face has lost its beauty.
> I have tossed and turned so many times that I am too tired
>   to leave my bed.
> It is not that I mind the others seeing
>   How ugly I have grown;
> It is you who have caused me to lose my beauty,
>   Yet it is you I am ashamed should see me!

Chang went away without meeting her, and a few days afterwards, when he was leaving the town, wrote a poem of final farewell, which said:

> You cannot say that you are abandoned and deserted;
>   For you have found some one to love you.
> Why do you not convert your broodings over the past
>   Into kindness to your present husband?

After that they never heard of one another again. Many of Chang's contemporaries praised the skill with which he extricated himself from this entanglement.

Hearing that His Friend
Was Coming Back from the War

By Wang Chien (*circa* A. D. 830)

In old days those who went to fight
In three years had one year's leave.
But in *this* war the soldiers are never changed;
They must go on fighting till they die on the battle-field.
I thought of you, so weak and indolent,
Hopelessly trying to learn to march and drill.
That a young man should ever come home again
Seemed about as likely as that the sky should fall.
Since I got the news that you were coming back,
Twice I have mounted to the high hall of your home.
I found your brother mending your horse's stall;
I found your mother sewing your new clothes.
I am half afraid; perhaps it is not true;
Yet I never weary of watching for you on the road.
Each day I go out at the City Gate
With a flask of wine, lest you should come thirsty.
Oh that I could shrink the surface of the World,
So that suddenly I might find you standing at my side.

314

The South

By Wang Chien

In the southern land many birds sing;
Of towns and cities half are unwalled.
The country markets are thronged by wild tribes;
The mountain-villages bear river-names.
Poisonous mists rise from the damp sands;
Strange fires gleam through the night-rain.
And none passes but the lonely fisher of pearls
Year by year on his way to the South Sea.

A Protest in the Sixth Year of Ch'ien Fu [A.D. 879]

By *Ts'ao Sung* (*flourished circa* A. D. 870-920)

The hills and rivers of the lowland country
　　You have made your battle-ground.
How do you suppose the people who live there
　　Will procure "firewood and hay"?[1]
Do not let me hear you talking together
　　About titles and promotions;
For a single-general's reputation
　　Is made out of ten thousand corpses.

[1] The necessaries of life.

Autumn

By Ou-yang Hsiu (b. 1007; d. 1072)

MASTER OU-YANG was reading his books[1] at night when he heard a strange sound coming from the north-west. He paused and listened intently, saying to himself: "How strange, how strange!" First there was a pattering and rustling; but suddenly this broke into a great churning and crashing, like the noise of waves that wake the traveller at night, when wind and rain suddenly come; and where they lash the ship, there is a jangling and clanging as of metal against metal.

Or again, like the sound of soldiers going to battle, who march swiftly with their gags[2] between their teeth, when the captain's voice cannot be heard, but only the tramp of horses and men moving.

I called to my boy, bidding him go out and see what noise this could be. The boy said: "The moon and stars are shining; the Milky Way glitters in the sky. Nowhere is there any noise of men. The noise must be in the trees."

[1] The poem was written in A. D. 1052, when Ou-yang was finishing his "New History of the T'ang Dynasty". [2] Pieces of wood put in their mouths to prevent their talking.

317

"I-hsi! alas!" I said, "this must be the sound of Autumn. Oh, why has Autumn come? For as to Autumn's form, her colours are mournful and pale. Mists scatter and clouds withdraw. Her aspect is clean and bright. The sky is high and the sunlight clear as crystal. Her breath is shivering and raw, pricking men's skin and bones; her thoughts are desolate, bringing emptiness and silence to the rivers and hills. And hence it is that her whisperings are sorrowful and cold, but her shouts are wild and angry. Pleasant grasses grew soft and green, vying in rankness. Fair trees knit their shade and gave delight. Autumn swept the grasses and their colour changed; she met the trees, and their boughs were stripped. And because Autumn's being is compounded of sternness, therefore it was that they withered and perished, fell and decayed. For Autumn is an executioner,[1] and her hour is darkness. She is a warrior, and her element is metal. Therefore she is called 'the doom-spirit of heaven and earth';[2] for her thoughts are bent on stern destruction.

"In Spring, growth; in Autumn, fruit: that is Heaven's plan. Therefore in music the note *shang* is the symbol of the West and *I-tsē* is the pitch-pipe of the seventh month. For *shang* means 'to strike'; when things grow old they are stricken by grief. And *I* means 'to slay'; things that have passed their prime must needs be slain. Plants and trees have no feelings; when their time comes they are blown down.

[1] Executions took place in autumn. See *Chou Li*, Book xxxiv (Biot's translation, tom. ii, p. 286).
[2] "Book of Rites", I. 656 (Couvreur's edition).

But man moves and lives and is of creatures most divine. A hundred griefs assail his heart, ten thousand tasks wear out his limbs, and each inward stirring shakes the atoms of his soul. And all the more, when he thinks of things that his strength cannot achieve or grieves at things his mind cannot understand, is it strange that cheeks that were steeped in red should grow withered as an old stick, and hair that was black as ebony should turn as spangled as a starry sky? How should ought else but what is fashioned of brass or stone strive to outlast the splendour of a tree? Who but man himself is the slayer of his youth? Why was I angered at Autumn's voice?"

The boy made no answer: he was sleeping with lowered head. I could hear nothing but the insects chirping shrilly on every side as though they sought to join in my lamentation.

The Pedlar of Spells

By Lu Yu (A. D. 1125-1210)

An old man selling charms in a cranny of the town wall.
He writes out spells to bless the silkworms and spells to
    protect the corn.
With the money he gets each day he only buys wine.
But he does not worry when his legs get wobbly,
For he has a boy to lean on.

The Herd-Boy

By Lu Yu

In the southern village the boy who minds the ox
With his naked feet stands on the ox's back.
Through the hole in his coat the river wind blows;
Through his broken hat the mountain rain pours.
On the long dyke he seemed to be far away;
In the narrow lane suddenly we were face to face.

The boy is home and the ox is back in its stall;
And a dark smoke oozes through the thatched roof.

Boating in Autumn

By Lu Yu

Away and away I sail in my light boat;
My heart leaps with a great gust of joy.
Through the leafless branches I see the temple in the wood;
Over the dwindling stream the stone bridge towers.
Down the grassy lanes sheep and oxen pass;
In the misty village cranes and magpies cry.

Back in my home I drink a cup of wine
And need not fear the greed[1] of the evening wind.

[1] Which "eats" men

How I Sailed on the Lake
Till I Came to the Eastern Stream

By Lu Yu

Of Spring water,—thirty or forty miles:
In the evening sunlight,—three or four houses.
Youths and boys minding geese and ducks:
Women and girls tending mulberries and hemp.
The place,—remote: their coats and scarves old:
The year,—fruitful: their talk and laughter gay.
The old wanderer moors his flat boat
And staggers up the bank to pluck wistaria flowers.

323

On the Birth of His Son

By *Su Tung-p'o* (*A. D. 1036–1101*)

Families, when a child is born
Want it to be intelligent.
I, through intelligence,
Having wrecked my whole life,
Only hope the baby will prove
Ignorant and stupid.
Then he will crown a tranquil life
By becoming a Cabinet Minister.

The Little Cart

A Seventeenth-Century Chinese Poem by Ch'ēn Tzŭ-lung

The following song describes the flight of a husband and wife from a town menaced by the advancing Manchus. They find the whole country-side deserted.

The little cart jolting and banging through the yellow haze
    of dusk.
  The man pushing behind: the woman pulling in front.
They have left the city and do not know where to go.
"Green, green, those elm-tree leaves: *they* will cure my hunger,
If only we could find some quiet place and sup on
    them together."
      The wind has flattened the yellow mother-wort:
      Above it in the distance they see the walls of a house.
"*There* surely must be people living who'll give you
    something to eat."
They tap at the door, but no one comes: they look in,
    but the kitchen is empty.
They stand hesitating in the lonely road and their tears
    fall like rain.

Ch'ēn Tzŭ-lung was born in 1607. He became a soldier, and in 1637 defeated the rebel, Hsü Tu. After the suicide of the last Ming emperor, he offered his services to the Ming princes who were still opposing the Manchus. In 1647 he headed a conspiracy to place the Ming prince Lu on the throne. His plans were discovered and he was arrested by Manchu troops. Escaping their vigilance for a moment, he leapt into a river and was drowned.

This volume, illustrated and decorated by Cyrus LeRoy Baldridge, was planned by Richard Ellis and produced under his direction. It was composed in a special Monotype cutting of Frederic W. Goudy's Deepdene type made for this edition, with swash letters and revised characters designed by Mr Ellis and with the approval of Mr Goudy. The paper, patterned after old papers of the orient, was manufactured by the P. H. Glatfelter Company, Spring Grove, Pennsylvania. The full-color illustrations were reproduced in Similetone by the Zeese-Wilkinson Company, Long Island City, New York. The cloth, in a natural finish, was made by Bancroft Mills, Wilmington, Delaware. The Composition, Electrotyping, Printing and Binding were by The Haddon Craftsmen, Camden, New Jersey.